T0077942

Why Is This Happening to Me?

❖ ❖ ❖ ❖ ❖

A Guide for Learning and Practicing Emotional Intelligence

Kathleen Kelly

BALBOA.PRESS

A DIVISION OF HAY HOUSE

Balboa Press books may be ordered through booksellers or by contacting:

Balboa Press
A Division of Hay House
1663 Liberty Drive
Bloomington, IN 47403
www.balboapress.com
844-682-1282

Because of the dynamic nature of the Internet, any web addresses or links contained in
this book may have changed since publication and may no longer be valid. The views
expressed in this work are solely those of the author and do not necessarily reflect the
views of the publisher, and the publisher hereby disclaims any responsibility for them.

The author of this book does not dispense medical advice or prescribe the use of any
technique as a form of treatment for physical, emotional, or medical problems without the
advice of a physician, either directly or indirectly. The intent of the author is only to offer
information of a general nature to help you in your quest for emotional and spiritual well-
being. In the event you use any of the information in this book for yourself, which is your
constitutional right, the author and the publisher assume no responsibility for your actions.

Any people depicted in stock imagery provided by Getty Images are models,
and such images are being used for illustrative purposes only.
Certain stock imagery © Getty Images.

Print information available on the last page.

ISBN: 978-1-9822-7399-6 (sc)
ISBN: 978-1-9822-7400-9 (e)

Balboa Press rev. date: 09/02/2021

Contents

About the Author

Kathleen has been reading self-help and spiritual books her entire adult life. Topics have included personal growth, improving relationships, human behavior, mental health, leadership, emotional intelligence, managing people, spiritual development, spiritual philosophies, and more. As a Program Manager, she has worked with and motivated people for over twenty years. She has also mentored younger people at various stages in their careers. She was moved after reading three books written by Daniel Goleman on emotional intelligence and believes, with Goleman, that teaching emotional intelligence in schools would add value to the overall learning experience. She decided to write a book that she could use to mentor young people who are starting their careers as well as to teach emotional intelligence.

Kathleen was born and raised in St. Louis, Missouri, the Show-Me state. She was raised in the Catholic religion and attended an all-girls Catholic high school. She obtained a Bachelor's Degree in Meteorology at St. Louis University and a Master's Degree in Atmospheric Science at the University of Missouri-Columbia. Kathleen worked for the federal government for thirty-five years as an operational Meteorologist, a research Meteorologist, a Program Manager, an Acquisition Manager, a Chief of Staff, a CIO, and an IT Security Compliance Officer. She retired from the federal government and worked in private industry as a Program Manager for thirteen more years.

In several books that Kathleen read, the authors used personal experiences to illustrate their points. Knowing that people always like a good story, she decided that a good way to teach emotional intelligence would be to describe her own experiences that relate to aspects of emotional intelligence. She hopes that people can relate to them and think about how they would demonstrate emotional intelligence in their own similar experiences.

Kathleen lives with her family of two cats in Annapolis, Maryland. She retired in April 2020 and is enjoying her favorite activities. She enjoys outdoor activities such as gardening, kayaking, biking, and hiking. Her love of music keeps her interested in playing the piano and Celtic harp.

Acknowledgments

I so appreciate my best friend from high school's review with edits and comments. Her advice from a teacher's perspective was invaluable. She kept me honest when I went astray. Her suggestion to add "gold nuggets" and headers for organization were also helpful. I even used a couple of her stories. It means a lot to me that she took the time to read and comment on my draft and that she is committed to the same cause as I am.

Preface

I was a Program Manager for the federal government for twenty-five-plus years as both a federal employee and a contractor. Before that, I was an operational Meteorologist and a research Meteorologist for twenty years. I have held many jobs during the past twenty-five years and an especially high number of jobs as a contractor in the past thirteen years. I experienced many managers who did not have emotional intelligence. Others and I suffered because of it. In 2014 and 2015, I was terminated from two jobs and resigned from one. In 2015, when my task ended in July, the government managers I worked with/for asked me to stay. The company they asked to hire me did so, but they really didn't want me. So they terminated me after a month. After that, I was unemployed as a Program Manager for over a year. I applied for so many jobs I lost count. I had numerous interviews, none of which resulted in employment. During this time of unemployment, I reflected, "Why is this happening to me?"

My friend Lauren said that I should create my next job, and when it comes, I should give out only positive vibes so that job lasts. This seemed oversimplified to me, as I liked the last three jobs that I was terminated from. I didn't think I did anything but work hard and follow best practices for management that I had learned through the years. My monthly horoscope (Susan Miller) said that I have had a rough seven years (as a Libra) and that was about to end. I was about to start the best year of my life. So, was it my destiny in the stars? My spiritual reading told me that I needed to picture myself in the job of my dreams and it would be manifested. I needed to pray to the Universe and the angels, and they would answer my prayers. My scientific training and readings in psychology told me that maybe it isn't all about me. Maybe, because of my career field, I have met with the type of people who are not trained in emotional intelligence and use ego and control as a means to get what they want. And maybe it is a combination of all these things. One thing I know is that I need to work on myself and be the best I can be. On that, I *do* have control.

I eventually started working at exactly the right time at exactly the right place in the best job for me. I enjoyed my last job, the one I retired from, and the people I worked with. I reflect back on my time off and what I accomplished during that time, and I am grateful. (I completed writing this book during my time off). I am grateful I ended my career with a good job I was happy with.

Introduction

Today's media is constantly bombarding us with stories of people acting out of hatred. To me, the "news" is just reports of humans misbehaving. Our politicians tell us that they will protect us from harm, whatever harm they choose to describe as threatening us. At work we face people with personal agendas who try to discredit or undermine us to get their way. Our marriages and friendships end, and we are at a loss for meaningful companionship. At times it seems like we are in a pressure cooker of emotions that could explode at any moment. How do we live in a fear-based society and keep our sanity? How do we react to the constant destructive emotions we experience either inside of us or from others? The answer is emotional intelligence.

Exactly what is emotional intelligence? Daniel Goleman, who wrote books on the subject, defined it as "being able…to rein in emotional impulse; to read another's innermost feelings; to handle relationships smoothly—as Aristotle put it, the rare skill 'to be angry with the right person, to the right degree, at the right time, for the right purpose, and in the right way.'"

If I had to describe emotional intelligence in one word, it would be *understanding*. To explain further, emotional intelligence is a combination of self-awareness and an understanding of the feelings you and others are having and why. Practicing emotional intelligence means acting on this knowledge and understanding. Practicing emotional intelligence results in compassion for yourself and others because you understand the feelings involved. It enables you to control and temper strong emotions that could hurt someone, including yourself. The old sayings "Walk a mile in my shoes" and "Do unto others as you would have others do unto you" both

1

are practices of emotional intelligence. They involve understanding and compassion.

What good is emotional intelligence to you? Practicing emotional intelligence helps you cope in this diverse world and enables you to let go of destructive emotions, such as anger, you might be harboring. It enables you to have healthy relationships. When you are a receiver of emotional intelligence, you feel listened to and valued. All these things bring happiness and peace in daily living.

We've all heard or seen the prayer, "God, grant me the serenity to accept the things I cannot change, courage to change the things I can, and wisdom to know the difference." Emotional intelligence is the ability to avoid experiencing destructive emotions as a result of circumstances over which we have no control. It is recognizing when we have the power to make changes that can benefit ourselves and others. Wisdom comes from understanding "Why this is happening to me" and what to do about it.

Adam Grant says in his book *Think Again*:

> "On Seinfeld, George Costanza famously said, "It's not a lie if you believe it." I might add that it doesn't become the truth just because you believe it. It's a sign of wisdom to avoid believing every thought that enters your mind. It's a mark of emotional intelligence to avoid internalizing every feeling that enters your heart."

Teaching children religion or some type of moral behavior or ethics is a good source of emotional intelligence training. Morals teach us rules for living in society with others. Christian morals include respect and consideration of others. Similarly, all the major world religions, including Islam, Judaism, Buddhism, and Hinduism, include moral behavior or ethics based on loving God and others in their teachings. Respect and consideration are the first step in learning and practicing emotional intelligence because they are motivation to understand others. But as our population grows and resources become limited, our society is turning more toward a me-first culture. More and more people are resorting to narcissism to help them cope or survive. Emotional intelligence promotes win-win encounters.

Parents who have emotional intelligence pass down the views and practices of emotional intelligence. But not all children grow up with emotionally intelligent parents. And sometimes when we get to be adults, we abandon the religion, and sometimes the morals, that we grew up with. That is why learning and practicing emotional intelligence at all ages is important for an individual's growth and mental and physical health. The mind, the body, and the soul are all intertwined. Emotions are an expression of the combination of thoughts from the mind and feelings from the soul. We cannot help what we feel, but we can control our emotions and expressions of those emotions using emotional intelligence. Daniel Goleman says, "Emotional learning is lifelong" (*Working with Emotional Intelligence*).

After reading Daniel Goleman's books on emotional intelligence, I felt that the practice of teaching emotional intelligence to elementary school children to create a complete package for their growth made total sense. There is much more to learning about and living life than reading, writing, and arithmetic. Suicide is now the second highest killer of teenagers today. This implies that we are letting our collective youth down in some way.

In this book, I quote a number of authors whose works I have read and who illustrate and support my points of view. One of these authors is Adam Grant, author of *Think Again*. He discusses many of the points I make in this book, but he does not connect them to emotional intelligence. Instead, I believe he presents a narrow view of emotional intelligence. This is what he says:

> "Instead of arguing about *whether* emotional intelligence is meaningful, we should be focusing on the contingencies that explain *when* it's more and less consequential. It turns out that emotional intelligence is beneficial in jobs that involve dealing with emotions, but less relevant--and maybe even detrimental--in work where emotions are less central."

Grant only discusses and provides data on emotional intelligence in the context of jobs, claiming that IQ is more than twice as important as emotional intelligence in predicting job performance. I agree. Emotional intelligence, on the other hand, is not a tool for forecasting job performance. We all have emotions all the time! Some we are not conscious of; others we can't hide. There are no jobs where emotions are more important than others. We all have emotions, no matter what job we have! Emotions are an essential component of the human psyche. Emotional intelligence refers to how we interpret our own and others' emotions, as well as what we do about them.

The purpose of this book is to educate the reader on achieving and practicing emotional intelligence in everyday life. I use real-life experiences to illustrate methods of using emotional intelligence to react or deal with difficult encounters. I share some of my own experiences in the hope that the reader will relate and learn from them as I did. Self-help books help you grow and become a better person. But once you work on yourself, you still have to deal with other people unless you become a hermit. So what do you do if you encounter other people who have not developed emotional intelligence? This book presents real-life situations that I and others have experienced when encountering emotionally immature people and what the best course of action was. Caroline Myss said in *Sacred Contracts*:

> "An old Zen saying has it, 'Before enlightenment, chop wood and carry water. After enlightenment, chop wood and carry water.' Heeding the call of the Divine within does not mean retiring to a life of contemplation in the mountains of Nepal or a cabin in the north woods... Today's mystics are more likely to continue to live in the material world but with an entirely different orientation and set of values—a challenge that can easily be as rigorous as any cloistered life."

The audience of this book, I assumed, would be mentally healthy adults. I don't have the training or expertise to help the mentally ill. I do present stories about mentally ill people who were in positions of influence in the workplace because it is important that we all recognize types of mental illness and how to deal with mentally ill people we encounter. I believe that there is much more mental illness in the world than we either know about or acknowledge. There is a fine line between mental illness and emotionally immature people. But most people who are mentally ill are emotionally immature.

This book, by far, is not all inclusive of the information available on emotional intelligence and enlightenment. There are many, many books written on each element I present. The purpose of this book is to highlight some of the major aspects of each topic I present and provide references for you to delve deeper into the various topics if you so choose.

The Ego

Any understanding of ourselves or human nature *has* to begin with a discussion of ego. The ego is comprised of what we think of ourselves and our stream of conscious thoughts about how we relate to our surroundings. A certain amount of acting on our ego is necessary for our survival, but when our ego is in control, we run the risk of losing sight of reality and inflating (or deflating) our view of ourselves. We run the risk of becoming narcissistic and exclusive. This, in turn, can result in paranoia and fear—fear that someone will take away what you consider to be yours and fear that someone different from you will harm you in some way. Eckhart Tolle says in his book *The Power of Now*:

> "As long as you are identified with your mind, the ego runs your life." And, "Identification with the mind… creates a false self, the ego, as a substitute for your true self rooted in Being…The ego's needs are endless. It feels vulnerable and threatened and so lives in a state of fear and want."

From what Tolle said, you can deduce that one can control his/her mind (thoughts) and, therefore, his/her ego.

I know we have all encountered someone who thinks more highly of himself/herself than others do of him/her. We label such people as egotistical or egomaniacs. We have all seen that the people with big egos are usually too busy promoting themselves to learn about and understand others. They spend an inordinate amount of time promoting themselves rather than listening to others' success stories. In the workplace, these people don't make the effort to consider the value of others and include them in decision making or problem solving. Deep down, though, those people are usually afraid of something. You will never get to know what because their behavior drives you away.

I think I have caused problems for myself because I am not impressed by braggadocios. To me, their words say nothing. People gain my respect when they act out of character and emotional intelligence. At work, people could sense when I didn't buy into the façade they were projecting. That caused them to either go on the attack or avoid me. I understand they are acting out of fear. My response is to always be the best I can be and to try to understand the other's point of view.

At one time, I worked for a large federal agency Chief Information Officer (CIO). The CIO was quite a braggadocio. He claimed to have invented the Internet and told his story whenever he had a new audience. No one believed him; instead they were quite amused at his fantasy. Although he knew very little about how to manage an Information Technology (IT) organization, he knew very well how to manipulate the new politicals at the highest level in the agency and win their favor. The career IT personnel, including me, had a hard time accepting his uninformed management style since we all had been there, faithfully doing our jobs and doing them well, before he came in. This man did little to win the respect of his subordinates, who found it hard to take him seriously. I would think that when a new manager comes into a preexisting organization, s/he would try to win the trust and respect of the organization employees. Promoting himself/herself with exaggerated stories is not the way to go about it.

I enjoyed my last job as a contractor Project Manager for a federal agency in a very visible program. The government Program Manager managed with emotional intelligence. He listened to his staff (and contractors) and made decisions based on what he learned from them and from his managers. You could always rely on him to speak the truth. He and I were a good team and I did a lot of extra work to help him succeed. Then there were organizational changes in the agency. The Program Manager was removed and replaced with a friend of one of the agency Deputy Directors. The new Program Manager was thirty-something and had no qualifications for the position and no past experience managing a Program. His behavior indicated that he managed with his ego rather than with emotional intelligence. Soon after he assumed the position, he asked the program staff for feedback on the mission, vision, and values he had drafted. Most likely, I was the only person who provided him feedback. He called me into his office and tore apart every single one of my comments with the purpose of demeaning me. Although I had already worked in the program for almost three years and he was new to the program, he refused to acknowledge or accept what I had learned in those three years about the program and its staff and conveyed to him in my feedback. He was very defensive and confrontational. Luckily, another manager entered his office after a while. He then told me, in a commanding voice, "We will continue this later." I knew that would never happen. Although I left his office in shock, I was grateful that I learned early on that he lacked emotional intelligence. He acted as though he was better than and more knowledgeable than everyone else, even though his Ph.D. degree was in a discipline totally unrelated to the work conducted in the program. He obviously did not welcome feedback on his draft even though he had asked for it. That was the last time I talked to him before I retired. What a contrast to the previous Program Manager!

Marianne Williamson quotes *A Course in Miracles* in her book *Return to Love*:

> "We think that without the ego, all would be chaos; the
> opposite is true. Without the ego, all would be love."

These words provide a lot to think about. Imagine what would happen if bosses who are obviously egotistical stopped acting out of their ego. They might start supporting their employees and the mission at hand. They might start showing compassion and understanding. This would create a culture in the workplace of respect for one another. We might all start enjoying working together!

The following quote from *A Course in Miracles* in Marianne Williamson's book, *A Return to Love*, describes why honoring the ego restricts our growth and openness to understanding others:

> "The ego bases its perception of reality on what has
> happened in the past, carries those perceptions into

the present and thus creates a future like the past. Past, present, and future are not continuous, unless you force continuity upon them."

You can see why this seems to go against what we take for granted—that we learn from the past and apply the lessons learned in the future. I would say that we need to balance learning and applying wisdom and keeping an open mind. For example, I never knew how my mother would react to something that I did or that happened to me. When I assumed she would act the same way as she did the last time I told her something about me, she acted the opposite way. When I told her, one time, I was changing jobs, she said, "Again? Why do you have to keep moving?" The next time I told her, she said, "I am happy for you." When I braced myself to hear the worst—condemnation, I was pleasantly surprised. When I was excited to tell her the good news, I faced judgment. So I could never predict how my mother would respond to what I told her. I could never assume that I knew her or totally understood her thinking.

When I was a Program Manager and hired a young African American woman to be my Program Coordinator, it turned out to be a disaster. She had no interest in the job. She spent much of her day on the phone with personal calls and e-mailing her friends. When I asked her to do something, it might or might not get done. If I had let that experience influence me, I would not have hired another African American woman in her place. But I did, and she turned out to be a good friend to this day. My first husband was an Electrical Engineer. He seemed so clueless and out of touch with life and reality. He constantly read science-fiction books to escape. He seemed unable to connect with another person on a deep, soulful level. I worked with predominantly clueless engineers during my career. They seemed so caught up in matters of the ego and were disinterested in matters of the souls of their subordinates or coworkers. I swore never to date or marry an engineer again. Then I met John. He had toured all over Europe after college, had spent a lot of time with the Maharishi Mahesh Yogi learning Transcendental Meditation (TM) in India, and practiced and taught TM. When I met him, I told him, "I never knew an enlightened engineer before!" He was proof that not all engineers were clueless to matters of the soul.

The government is making training in hidden biases available for federal employees. Hidden biases are a result of what Marianne Williamson described in her quote above—projecting the ego's perceptions of reality into the future. Preventing our ego from forming biases based on past experiences or generalizations is part of the work necessary for emotional intelligence. It is interesting and admirable that the federal government is including training related to this aspect of emotional intelligence as part of Equal Employment Opportunity (EEO) programs. But that training only reaches a small contingency of the total working population. In his book, *Think Again*, Adam Grant quotes psychologist Elizabeth Krumrei Mancuso and her colleagues: "Learning requires the humility to realize one has something to learn." How many people have you come across in your career who thought they were finished learning in high school or college and thought they knew everything?

Steve Hagen said in *Buddhism Plan and Simple*:

> "It's imperative that our dissatisfaction originates within us. It arises out of our own ignorance, out of our blindness to what our situation actually is, out of wanting reality to be something other than what it is. Our longing, our craving, our thirsting for something other than reality is what dissatisfies us.

So the expression, "You are your worst enemy," is true. We cause many of our own problems by wanting and not letting go.

I had an old picture of a woman, probably from the twenties, that I inherited from my grandmother. The saying under the picture said, "A woman wants for little here below and wants that little long." It is a clever play on words that means we are always wanting for something; when we get it, we immediately want something else. Wanting and dissatisfaction are products of the ego.

There are many books on the ego and how it can make trouble for you. Many of them are spiritual books on different Asian spiritual philosophies. Others are self-help books on relationships and how to suppress the ego when trying to develop and maintain a relationship. A book whose title caught my eye in the local library catalog was a book by the Dalai Lama entitled *How to See Yourself as You Really Are.* I think that would be a good book to read next.

The main thing is that we need to ignore the subconscious stream of thought that tells us that we are better or more right than others—or less and can't do anything right. We need to ignore the internal tapes that tell us that we aren't good enough. We need to overcome the thoughts that are harmful to us and others, such as fear, selfishness, paranoia, and so on. We need to, instead, embrace the openness and thoughtfulness that allows us to feel respect and compassion for all people. After all, we are all connected, imperfect human beings. We can use meditation as a means of controlling the thoughts of the mind and opening it up to love. In *The Gift of Change*, Marianne Williamson said:

> "As we humble ourselves and step back with our ego, allowing God to lead the way, miracles occur naturally. No stress, no strain."

Know and Understand Your Cultural Influences (United States)

I learned a lot about society and culture in the United States from experience, of course, but also from authors like Erich Fromm, Jimmy Carter, and Al Gore. I really enjoyed Al Franken's books, which educated me on politics in the United States using humor. All of these books had powerful messages that I won't forget.

To understand who and what you are, you must first understand your cultural influences. Many of these influences we take for granted. For example, I grew up in a middle-class homogeneously white neighborhood. I attended a Catholic parish grade school and an all-girl Catholic high school. I was taught at these schools to keep growing and be the best you can be. When I got out in the work world, I assumed everyone thought like I did. Big mistake! Not all people strive to keep growing and be the best they can be. In fact, many people resent people who keep growing and feel they are shown up by them. Many are content with mediocrity or behave as if they stopped maturing when they were in their early twenties.

The human being is such a complex entity because his/her personality is determined by inherited genes, character learned from his/her family and developed from life's experiences, education, and influences of his/her environments from local to national. Whether you are conscious of it or not, each of these things makes you the unique person that you are. A person's growth is either encouraged or inhibited by his/her environments and the number of different environments s/he experiences. For example, educational environments such as colleges can stimulate growth in not just subject knowledge but in emotions and in reasoning. At St. Louis University, a private Jesuit college where I got my bachelor's degree, two religion courses were mandatory. In one of them, the Jesuit priest made reading a book on atheism mandatory for the course. Some of the premises of the book made sense to me, and I stopped going to church for a long time after reading the book. A person's growth living in a ghetto with little chances of experiencing other environments will be limited and can be stunted so that his/her behavior changes little from the time s/he is a teen. Some people choose to overcome a lot of the growth-limiting factors in their environment and become the person they want to be. My friend Mary moved from South Carolina to Washington D.C. for a higher paying job. She left a family environment that discouraged her growth and, in fact, suppressed her. She overcame a lot to escape that environment and has grown tremendously since making the move.

It has been said that the people today carry the burden of what happened to their ancestors in the past. For example, African Americans carry the burden of their slave predecessors who endured emotional trauma and physical abuse. Jewish Americans carry the burden of the atrocities committed against the Jews by Hitler. There is no escaping the influence that such major historical events have on people as a group. This means that if your people's history tends to limit your growth, you must identify and overcome these factors to reach your full potential.

One of the keys to happiness and contentment is that, once you understand what made you what you are, you must accept and work with those things. You must use your experiences as a means of learning and growing. You must turn negative experiences into opportunities for growth, making lemonade from lemons. Maybe your parents told you that difficult experiences teach you character, like my mother used to tell me.

During one summer, in the evenings, I binge-watched *Mad Men* on Netflix. I see why it was so popular. To me, it illustrates all the pressures a person experiences from his/her culture in each of his/her roles: spouse, parent, child, sibling, employee, manager, citizen, group member, caretaker, and so on. In society, we are usually juggling several different roles. Sometimes one or more roles place huge pressures on us that we don't even realize. We just keep playing our roles, trying to keep our heads above water. Sometimes we fail. Hopefully, then, it isn't too late to change something in our lives to understand what happened, determine a resolution, and fix any damage we did. Sometimes we want to escape our situation and do something new and different. Sometimes we make a bad choice and hurt ourselves or someone else. Don Draper was under tremendous pressure to perform as a husband, father, and manager in a demanding job. Sometimes he coped with that pressure by seeking solace in different women. Sometimes he made bad choices. Don's wife, Betty, was also under tremendous pressure to run the household, raise her children, serve as a citizen of good standing, and serve and be faithful to her husband. The series is also a good depiction of life and philosophies of the late fifties and early sixties. It makes the viewer realize the advancements or changes in philosophies that have occurred since then. While Betty was pregnant with her third child, she never stopped smoking and drinking wine. A woman's place was in the home; if she worked outside the home, she was usually in a position that served a man or men. Professional women had to constantly prove themselves worthy of their positions. The series is a great illustration of human nature and cultural influences. Betty tried to fit in activities that fed her soul, such as horseback riding. Don, on the other hand, more often suppressed the needs of his soul except when he disappeared for several weeks to visit people in his past in California and take time to do some soul searching and find answers. He came out of that experience with renewed appreciation for his wife and family. After Don and Betty's divorce, Don hit rock bottom before he started back on his way up. He wrote and organized his thoughts in a journal. Neither Don nor Betty was happy when they suppressed the needs of their souls. When they suppressed the needs of their souls, they usually sought solace in people outside their family. Emotional intelligence helps us live a happier life and keep ourselves on more of an even keel. It helps us to accept reality and then make the best of it. In season 4, episode 7, Don Draper was writing in his journal and narrated: "People tell us who they are, but we ignore them because we want them to be who we want them to be."

Remember the book *I'm OK—You're OK*? It was an attempt in the setting of the progressive sixties to tell people they should accept themselves and others. To understand your cultural influences, you must start at the highest level of U.S. society and work your way down to personal influences such as family and friends and where you grew up. This book does not address biological makeup, inherited genes, or ethnicity. You must get to know and understand their influences from family interactions.

Capitalism

If you want a true picture of the U.S. culture in which you live and which influences everything you do, read Erich Fromm's *Sane Society*. Erich Fromm is a renowned philosopher. His book *The Art of Loving* was mandatory reading for my English class in high school. Fromm wrote this book and several others in the early fifties. He is amazing. His books are not an easy read, but they are so accurate. It amazes me how relevant and applicable Fromm's description of U.S. society is today in the twenty-first century. In fact, things he described seem to have intensified and become more universal since the 1950s. I had an aha moment when I read *Sane Society* in my late fifties. It explained a lot of life and work experiences I had. I encourage others to read it at a younger age to help them understand how our society works and why people behave as they do.

The United States is the model capitalistic country, the model to which China aspires to be like, good or bad. To understand what capitalism means to you, we must start at the top—with society—and drill down to the individual. First of all, the goals of capitalism are production and consumption. We must produce, produce, produce and consume, consume, consume. A person's value is proportionate to his/her amount of production and consumption. Anyone who doesn't produce or consume is a useless drain on society. Economics is all about the balance of producing and consuming. One can't buy anything if s/he doesn't work and produce to enhance his/her buying power.

It's interesting how, during the (2020) pandemic, we in the United States became aware of some of capitalism's realities. People working in service industries do not produce consumable goods; they have some of the lowest-paying jobs in the country. States are hesitant to raise the minimum wage because of the economic consequences. During the pandemic, however, we saw how reliant we all are on the services that service providers provide. We put up signs thanking them for their efforts. During the pandemic, many service providers were unable to work, causing them hardship. Many had no choice but to work, also causing them hardships. Many parents, exhausted from teaching their children while working full-time jobs, were suddenly extremely thankful for what teachers do. All persons supporting the operations within hospitals were suddenly appreciated and highly valued. It is also interesting how, post-pandemic, service providers are reluctant to return to their low-paying jobs, causing reductions in the services they provided. What will the future bring? Will the appreciation service providers were shown during the pandemic relate to higher pay for them post-pandemic? It is difficult to change a culture and people's mindset.

Also, during the pandemic, another reality of capitalism that became obvious is that the "American dream" is not afforded to everyone. Some people, especially those in service industries, can barely live day-to-day. While big industry managers have accumulated excessive amounts of wealth, the country's poorest can hardly afford to pay for groceries for their families. The gap between rich and poor has grown and is being ignored or worsened by the actions of some of our country's politicians. People in low-paying jobs were more vulnerable to the hardships the pandemic caused.

Big industries rule. Some of the biggest industries in the United States are oil, insurance, IT, medicine, pharmaceuticals, alcohol, banking, marketing, media, and road vehicles. Where would we be without our vehicle (car, SUV, or truck) which consumes oil and provides us the freedom to go where we want when we want? (I am happy to say that I am seeing more and more electric cars on the road). Our "ride" has all the latest technology so we can keep connected and communicate with others outside the vehicle while driving. Our vehicle takes us to stores where we buy what we need and/or want. Following the pandemic, there is a shortage of vehicles being manufactured due to a shortage of computer chips that are critical to today's vehicle operation. People are being inconvenienced during travel because rental companies sold their cars during the pandemic, resulting in a limited supply of rental cars.

The medical industry is helping more and more people to live longer and recover from body ailments than ever before. We are learning more and more about what sustains the body and what destroys it. Drugs are helping to control and/or suppress ailments and diseases to prolong life. New technology in the form of computers and robots is facilitating surgery and post-surgery patient care. There is so much knowledge now in the medical field that any one physician cannot know it all. Therefore, if you develop an illness, you will most likely be referred to a specialist who knows all about that area and nothing else.

It's a good thing there are medical advancements because the insurance industry is slowly taking charge of the medical industry and restricting patient care time. For example, more surgery is being performed as outpatient care because hospital stays are becoming too costly, and insurance companies are refusing to pay. The type of insurance and provider you select and pay determine what type of and amount of care you get. Needless to say, a person who cannot afford health insurance has a higher chance of dying younger than his/her wealthy counterpart. Insurance can also help pay for the drugs you need to survive. Insurance companies can dictate what drugs you can and cannot get. For example, an insurance company may only pay for a generic drug instead of a more expensive brand-name drug. Again, only those who can afford these drugs or the insurance to cover the drugs can benefit. Many people who cannot afford the drugs they need to survive succumb. They succumb to both illness and capitalism's flaws.

The stronghold of the pharmaceutical industry is evidenced by the number of drug commercials on television. In between certain programs at certain times of the day, the number of drug commercials exceeds all other types of commercials. Physicians are rewarded with payment by pharmaceutical companies for pushing or prescribing their drugs to patients. So certain physicians will develop preferences for one type or brand of drug over the other. The norm appears to be that when a doctor diagnoses a disease, he assumes the patient will do nothing to change his/her behavior to cure that disease—that is, stop drinking or smoking, eat more greens, get more exercise, and so on. More often than not, the doctor is correct. Many times, though, the patient just doesn't have the wherewithal to change his/her behavior. For example, s/he may be too old or weak or does not have money to pay for more healthy food instead of the cheaper, less nourishing food so readily available. Many times, the patient does not ask the right questions and just trusts the doctor to decide what is good for him/her. This most often is because the patient does not have the knowledge or experience to ask the right questions. So the doctor prescribes a drug that will mask the symptoms and enable the patient to cope with the ailment. Use of drugs to cope with life is a subject I will touch on in a later chapter.

Another huge industry in the United States is the alcohol business. It is the universal drug for which one does not need a prescription. So many of my women friends are divorced from or are coping with an alcoholic husband. Many of the news reports of men's bad behaviors resulting in crime are due to them being high on drugs or alcohol. Just recently, Maryland passed a law in which the cars of any person convicted of his/ her first DUI or DWI will be equipped with breathalyzers, which disable the car's startup if the breathalyzer indicates alcohol content over the legal limit. This law was passed, in part, due to the person whose alcohol content was three times over the legal limit who ran over and killed Noah Leotta, a Montgomery County, Maryland, police officer who was on duty and who had pulled over a drunk driver. Drinking alcohol has been socially ingrained and accepted, as evidenced by widespread happy hours in restaurants, binge drinking at colleges, and the booming beer and wine industries. In many cases, drinking alcohol has been associated with having fun and enabling someone to escape the drudgery of life.

An industry that all other industries use and take advantage of is the marketing industry. Big industries advertise what they have to sell. I remember a time when there were no advertisements on the Internet. Now they are everywhere—in e-mail systems, on social media, in videos you download, and more. Television commercials are big. Super Bowl commercials are as big a deal as the game itself. Only the biggest industries can afford to advertise on television. Industries advertising heavily on television are the drug, automobile, and movie and television (media) industries. Television commercials barrage us with drug advice: "Be sure to ask your doctor about so-and-so drug; it could be the answer to your pain or ailment." During election years, politicians in political commercials tell us what they are going to do for us if elected and degrade their opponents. While commercials can provide knowledge of a new product to enhance our living, we must realize that the intent of commercials is to brainwash us and cause us to want and buy. Television stations like QVC can be addictive and cause us to spend money we don't have and buy things we really don't need, just because products offered are so inexpensive. An innate premise of capitalism is that competition is promoted—"all is fair in love and war" kind of thing.

Another change capitalism has brought to cultural norms is a change in loyalty. My father worked for the *St. Louis Post-Dispatch* for fifty years. He worked his way up from an errand boy as a teenager and retired as a copywriter. He worked with clients to determine how to sell their products and set up ads on newspaper pages. This job used both his analytical and artistic skills. Christmastime, the capitalists' best season, was stressful for him with all the corporations trying to bring joy to people during the season. Dad was loyal to the *Post-Dispatch*, and the *Post-Dispatch* was loyal to him. They took care of him through the years and promoted him to a job he was well suited for and was profitable for the company. That kind of loyalty does not exist in companies today. Today, it is common for people to stay in one job for one company three years or less. The name of the game is to find a job where there will be lasting work. I know in government support work, companies win and lose contracts. People working for one company in a government support job may find that, after a year, they are working for a different company that won the follow-on contract. In addition, if there is no work in your discipline, companies lay you off. Companies hire those who have the experience the position calls for. Training on the job is generally not a practice in private industry any longer.

Most offer letters today state that your employment by the company is "at will." This means that both parties, the company and the employee, must will to maintain the partnership. If, at any time, one of the parties wants to break the partnership, they can. More and more often, an employee has no qualms, after a year or less, moving to another company with a higher salary offer. More and more often, a company has no qualms about terminating an employee when they can replace him or her with an employee who will work for a lower salary. Less and less, companies and their employees take responsibility for each other. More and more, employees are there for the paycheck, and companies use employees as bodies to fill positions at the lowest possible compensation rate.

Lack of loyalty raises another issue with big businesses. As a company grows, it has less influence on the behavior of its employees. Training becomes less effective. Mentoring is rare (because it requires special attention and devoted time to a few). If employees are hired to fill a position and they aren't loyal to the company's mission and have a personal agenda to serve themselves first, the company is not represented in a favorable light. Take, for example, my encounters with my mother's phone company, which is a huge communications business. Since my mother was old and lost most of her eyesight, I took care of her business for her. When she fell and broke her hip and was no longer able to live alone, I arranged a place for her in a small assisted-living home. I called her phone company to terminate her landline phone service in her apartment and to set up new service in her room at the assisted-living home. I had requested her new service to begin on February 1. On February 2, it became obvious that she wouldn't be able to move to the home because she fell gravely ill. I called her phone company to suspend service until further notice. On February 6, she passed away, so I called her phone company to cancel her phone service at the new home. Now everything in her phone company is automated. Phone calls with her phone company representatives are recorded. Bills are automatically produced. If you make a change during a billing period, too bad. The automated bill goes out anyway, charging you for the next billing period without considering the change. I received two bogus bills for my dead mother, charging her for service she did not use. I tried multiple ways and times to reach company representatives to correct the charges and her bills to no avail. By talking to many different representatives, I was able to piece together what happened. Company representatives made six errors screwing up her new phone bill. One representative told me that they had no record of me calling them to suspend her new service. However, when I called to terminate it, the representative told me that she had to reinstate service and *upgrade* it. My mother's bill included charges to do so. The phone company never did terminate her old landline service, and they didn't change the billing address to my address as I had requested. Billing automatically kept sending new bills to her old address, which I did not receive since I did not forward her mail (since most of her mail was junk mail and charity requests for money). Finally the phone company terminated service because I did not pay any of the bills they kept sending my mother for service she did not and could not use.

I wrote two letters to the company CEO. The first one was a complaint about the bogus bills. An executive customer service representative called me to tell me that bills are not corrected until the second billing. What? You mean you cannot stop the wheels from turning in the wrong direction for a month? You mean that with all the automation, a click of the computer can't make an immediate change in a bill? I was incredulous but just said thank you and hung up. What she predicted did not happen. The billing situation just got worse until one day I decided I was going to keep calling the company until I got in touch with a representative who "got it" and could actually do something about it. On the third call, I finally got someone who got it and said she would manually change the bill. Yes, manually is what it takes. That was after I had two incredible conversations with several different representatives. One of the reps told me that my mother's bill for the new service was not bogus and kept going over the charges on the current bill, which was useless since the error occurred in the previous bill. I finally said, "I see you can't help me, thanks," and hung up. The second time, I explained what happened to the representative who said that she couldn't help me, that she would have to connect me with the Finance Department. I explained what happened to the Finance Department representative, and she said that she couldn't help me; she would have to transfer me to the Billing Department (which I had just talked to). Again I explained to the Billing Department what happened, and she said she had to transfer me to the Finance Department. I said, "I just talked to them, and they said that they would have to transfer me to you." Finally, I said, "I see you can't help me. Thank you," and hung up. Then I tried a different number. Jackpot! The representative who answered could actually *do* something.

Do you see a problem here? I wrote the company CEO a second letter telling him that he had a problem with training representatives. Many of them did not know what they were doing and made errors that screwed up customer orders. Many of them did not know how to fix things that other representatives or the automated billing system screwed up. Not everything can be automated and serve customers well. No surprise, I did not receive a response to my second letter even though I intended it to help the company and provide the top manager some insight to problem areas in his company.

To me this is a logical outcome of the growth of big business and the hiring of employees who are not trained well enough, not knowledgeable enough to properly help customers, not empowered, and not motivated enough to investigate customer issues until they are resolved. Everything is departmentalized, and it's the *other* department's responsibility. I believe that customer service cannot be fully automated; automation is a tool to facilitate tracking business records. As part of quality control, companies of all sizes need to ensure that their employees are empowered to do their jobs and are effective. Employees need to be able to investigate a faulty situation, analyze the results, and then make corrections. Merely reading scripts or mimicking canned responses to their customers is not enough.

Then there are the "safe" cameras every mile in some places in Montgomery County, MD. I was driving up I-95 past new construction to get to work for six months. The speed limit signs included a sign that said "Photo enforced." Never saw any cameras. Then one day in February, I saw a flash as I sped by. Uh oh. Several months passed, and I didn't receive a citation. I thought, "Phew. I escaped somehow." Then, three months later, I received a notice that the Maryland Vehicle Administration (MVA) had placed a flag on my car registration. I had to pay a fee and the citation fee in order to renew my registration. What citation? I called them. The MVA representative told me that they had mailed me the citation three times. Since I didn't pay the fine, the flag was placed on my registration. I told her I never received the citation. She said again, "It was mailed three times." But to whom? I'm sure I would have noticed something like that in the mail! How do you prove you did *not* get something in the mail? And it was obvious that the MVA rep was reading the words she was supposed to use in situations like that. She was powerless to do anything but say, "It was mailed three times." They had me. So I had to call and get the citation number, pay the citation fee and late fee, get the receipt, then go to the MVA and pay the flag fee, providing the receipt of citation fee payment, to get the flag removed from my registration. Only then was I able to renew my registration. I was mad. What a rip-off! Automation sometimes just doesn't cut it. I will never know where my citation was sent. I am not alone, though. My realtor said the same thing happened to him. So what do you do in a situation like that? You have no choice but to pay the fines and check with the MVA the next time you see a flashing camera alongside the road. The county's first concern appeared to be with making money. It failed to build in protection for the consumer when the contractor executing the program made a mistake. The consumer was assumed to be at fault for not paying the fine on time and had no recourse. The MVA representative was powerless to help the consumer.

A friend of mine told me about her experience with a large insurance company sales person. Her story indicated a similar problem. She had called and talked with an insurance company sales representative, and the representative could provide only limited information. So my friend decided to do her own research on the Internet. She found that the majority of reviews of that company provided stories of cases where they had to keep producing evidence and paperwork to prove that they deserved reimbursement. My friend wrote the sales representative she had talked to a very nice letter explaining that she had decided not to go with her company because she wanted to simplify her life, not complicate it with more paperwork and documentation to prove she was entitled to benefits. The representative wrote back a very short response, basically saying that no system is perfect and to let her know if she changed her mind. My friend was incredulous. She said, "This is sales?" I pointed out that the sales rep probably figured she had no power to change my friend's mind and to offer her any assurance that she would be treated as a special customer. And maybe rightly so. Maybe that is another negative outcome of working in a large capitalistic company. You are powerless, just as the MVA representative was powerless to do anything about my not receiving a citation. Company representatives feel powerless to invoke any positive change for the company, for the customer, or themselves. The result is mediocrity at best. People do what they are told to do in their job and don't think about things like how to improve their efficiency or the efficiency of the company.

I found that people feel powerless in a big organization in the federal government just as they do in big industry. When I was a federal employee, I found that the government, similar to a large company, is a huge machine or a big, inflexible steel wheel that keeps turning slowly and will run over you if you don't get out of the way. Everyone living in fear of the machine jumps on the wheel and turns with it for their own protection. Anyone who jumps off the wheel either because they do not like where it is going or have a suggestion for a better place to go is crushed.

I worked for the federal government for almost fifty years. It took me twenty years to realize that a large majority of federal workers lived and worked in fear. I only realized it once I became a manager. I was working in a large program whose mission was to acquire and deploy Doppler radars. Several of the top managers in the program had never managed an acquisition like that before and did not know how to manage well. They did things that had costly consequences to the program and the people in it. They did things that only promoted their own reputations and furthered their own agendas. At one point, my supervisor, who had a favorite support contractor, saw that this contractor's contract, which would be supporting my office, was renewed. The Contracting Officer sent me the Statement of Work (SOW) that my boss approved to make sure I agreed with the description of the technical work the contractor would be performing. I was shocked! The description was obviously written by someone who did not know government format or language. It was describing work that the contractor would be performing for me, but I had had no input into the description of the work in the SOW. I knew that the president of the company wrote the SOW and my boss sent it directly to the Contracting Officer for execution. This is unethical. Contractors are not to write their own SOW, for obvious reasons. I investigated what happened. I found that my boss told the president of the company to write up the SOW and send it to a "flunky" that worked for him. The flunky was supposed to review the SOW and put it into government format. But he did not know how to do this. My boss had no interest in this low-level work, so that is why he told Jose to do it. Jose was afraid to fall out of favor, so he sent the SOW to the Contracting Officer with only minor edits. I was appalled. I asked Jose why he did that. His response essentially told me that he was afraid of losing his job if he didn't do what the boss told him to do even though he knew it was not the right thing to do. A lightbulb went on in my head. I realized that many of the people in that program did the same thing. They were afraid of losing their jobs, so they did whatever the upper-level managers, who most of the time followed their own agendas, told them to do. And it is difficult to fire government employees! Still they were afraid of losing their jobs. They chose to work in an environment where they were suppressed and unhappy.

Technology

The United States is all about technology these days. We lived through the Industrial Revolution where industries produced widgets; now we produce and share information. We need IT to live day-to-day—we use our computers and mobile phones all day long to perform daily functions. Technology provides us the ability to communicate, document, photograph, and create and listen to music. When technology fails in the workplace, the workers are crippled and might as well go home. Technology in the manufacturing industry has enabled us to produce more with less (people). Technology is providing many job opportunities. The field of IT Security is wide open and provides more job opportunities by the day.

The Internet is an endless source of information. We can get instantaneous news and information from the Internet. We can obtain news that we don't even care to know about on the Internet. We can watch cat videos and videos of people doing amazing, even stupid things. Anything we need to know about we can look up on the Internet. I used to look up ailments and what to do about them on the Internet for my aged mother. Her general physician was essentially useless. Once he prescribed drugs for her that caused her to bleed internally. I said, "No more," so I monitored her health and took care of her myself using the information I looked up on the Internet. I looked up the side effects of any drugs her doctor prescribed for her and determined if she should take the risk. Usually, I advised against it, considering her age, and she agreed.

One use of the Internet that I particularly like is the ability to share information in a neighborhood. At one time I had two different houses in two different cities/neighborhoods. One was a weekend house. In the one neighborhood, we have a list-serve, which is a group of people who signed up and sent each other e-mails providing or requesting information. In the other neighborhood, we used Facebook to share and request information. Both vehicles served to make you feel that you are a part of a community and working for the good of that community.

Security has become increasingly important, since the use of the Internet has increased, and so have incidents from hackers and Internet thieves. Hackers are stealing personal information and identities every day from government organizations, stores, and corporations. IT Security is providing many new job opportunities. Many management jobs supporting the federal government in the IT discipline require a secret or top-secret clearance.

At the same time people are feeling more depersonalized, technology is working to help them. Or is it? Technology's answer to better living is the cell phone—that is, a cell phone that is always connected to the Internet, such as Androids and iPhones. No matter where you are, you can be connected to the Internet and, hence, to other people. People no longer have to rely on their memory to recall information. They can look it up on their cell phone. In crowds or on the street, people do not look at others or their surroundings; they look down at their phones. At restaurants, you see couples at a table, each person looking at his/her phone and typing. I wonder why they are even together when their focus is somewhere else with some other person. We no longer have to talk face-to-face. Texting, with abbreviations, has become a major means of communication rather than voice communication. Then we have social media. People can say whatever they want to without having to face the person s/he is talking to or about. That is very empowering. Someone who is invisible can make his/her voice heard to the world. But as it turns out, some people do not have very nice things to say. Many comments shared (by emotionally immature people) publicly are hateful and hurtful. We have bullying, both personal and on social media. Anyone considered different can easily become a target for bullying. In the workplace, bullying is a means to scare others into conforming to another's agenda or to the company culture.

Technology for music is constantly changing. Within fifty years, we listened to music on LP records, then tapes, then CDs. I found I had to keep spending more and more money to update my music media. I once told the sales rep at a store that sold electronics that I was tired of the continual changes in technology. He told me, "We have to do that to get you to spend money." I was satisfied with that honest answer. With the rise in Internet use, now we can download music of our choice anytime. Within the same fifty years, televisions have shrunk in depth to pretty much flat, increased in size, and decreased in cost. We can stream programs for television from the Internet by using a small "stick" inserted in the back of our televisions. We can download television programs we miss through the Internet. No need to rent or buy DVDs any longer. We can watch any movie we want to at any time using a streaming service. When we are in our road vehicles, we can talk on our cell phones without holding the cell phone through technology built into our vehicles. We can listen to the radio on the television. All of these advances in technology undeniably affect how we live day to day. Technology affects how we receive information and how we relate to other people.

Of course, with all the good that technology brings, there is the usual downside. Since the Internet is a type of media, we cannot believe everything we see or read on the Internet. For example, a friend of mine's sister had breast cancer. When she was going through her treatment and reconstruction, she spent a lot of time looking up procedures and medications on the Internet. She said her doctor recognized that she was doing that by the questions she was asking. He congratulated her for educating herself but cautioned her to use only two websites—Web MD or the Mayo Clinic—regarding medical things. He said there is too much bogus medical information on the Internet. Too many patients take things into their own hands by believing what they read on the Internet without talking to their doctor about it. They can cause serious harm to themselves as a result. It takes emotional intelligence to know and understand which Internet sources and information are reliable and accurate.

Another issue with the Internet is reviews. Sometimes reviews of a restaurant, product, or company are written by people with an underlying agenda. For example, I worked for a very bad small company. Numerous employees and ex-employees wrote scathing reviews about the company and its owners on Glassdoor, a website that provides the public company reviews and open job positions. These negative reviews prevented the company from being able to hire good employees in many cases. So the CEO decided that the company needed some positive reviews on Glassdoor. She wrote a couple reviews and had a couple favored employees write a couple, all in the same time period. A different employee, who recognized what was going on, wrote a review telling the public not to believe those reviews because they were written by the CEO. In another case, on public radio, I heard that at one time there was a "war" going on between two car dealerships. One was purposely discrediting the other on the Internet so that people would take their business to the dealer without bad reviews. I've noticed that sometimes, even restaurant reviews for restaurants I like can be a bit harsh, just because something happened that displeased the customer on that particular day. All of these examples tell us that the Internet is a source of a lot of information that we need to use with discretion. There are a lot of critics out there that may or may not provide us with accurate information. We need to use emotional intelligence when writing reviews and when discerning which are helpful and which have an underlying agenda.

Population Growth

The world is suffering (silently) from a large population growth. On the news one night, there was a story on how the Washington D.C. airport traffic has gotten so bad that city planners were trying to find solutions quickly for the summer vacation. The U.S. Park Service is trying to figure out how to handle the 50–60 percent increase in park visitors by staggering entrance times or capping the number of visitors in any day. The effects of a large population growth include competition for resources. Right now in the United States there is competition for jobs and housing. In parts of the western United States, there is competition for water, which can be heightened anywhere there is prolonged drought. The rich are getting richer, and the poor poorer. This means that there is a smaller group of people who want for nothing and a larger group who sometimes have trouble feeding and housing themselves and their families.

In the past, wars have been a means of population control. Large numbers of people were wiped out in wars—55 million in World War II. Terrorism and the fight against terrorism have replaced outright wars (except in the example of Syria). Natural disasters also wipe out large numbers of people in the form of earthquakes and cyclones. The number of people killed in a natural disaster is proportional to the population in the locality where the disaster strikes. During the COVID pandemic in 2020 and the first half of 2021, over 600,000 people died in the United States.

With the increase in population, there is an increase of people with mental illness and physical ailments. Of course, the strain on society is the increase of poor people who cannot afford treatment and cure of mental and physical illnesses. Many of these people are out on the streets with nowhere to go. Every day, it seems, someone in the United States snaps and shoots others and maybe himself. Usually these people have a mental imbalance of some kind. Sometimes people who harm others are on drugs or alcohol. The United States is divided in how to handle the increase of poor people who cannot care for themselves and members of their families. One philosophy is that we are all one nation and we need to take care of everyone in that nation. The opposite philosophy is that every man needs to take care of himself; those who take care of themselves should be rewarded. I believe that we need to wipe out ignorance and poverty by ensuring that everyone gets a minimal education and the wide opportunities that accompany it. This is easier said than done, which is precisely why it hasn't been done. Bernie Sanders, in his 2016 campaign for the Democratic presidential nominee, told young people that they are entitled to a free college education. This would cost the federal government a lot of money, and the conservatives would never go for it. For one thing, it would mean that there would be a more even distribution of resources, which goes against the premise of capitalism and the competition it promotes.

With an increase in population in a capitalistic culture, there is an increase in competition for resources and jobs. It is harder to get into colleges. It is harder to find a job that you are suitable for. The saying, "It's not what you know, it's who you know" is more relevant. Sometimes the job you are looking for could be filled by so many other people that you will not be noticed unless you know someone who can recommend you. When you want to travel somewhere, you have to plan way in advance and make reservations because there are so many people traveling to the same place at the same time. So as to not lose money, airlines fill all flights to capacity. Flights are sometimes cancelled if they are not filled. Traffic in large cities is bad most of the time in most of the places.

In the IT industry, for example, a lot of managers are required, managers who know what they are doing. But companies often hire managers who promote themselves as skilled and experienced only to find out that their new hires are not cutting it. Enter the Project Management Institute (PMI). PMI found a niche to make money. They came up with requirements for project and program managers and developed training so people could meet those requirements. They charge a high price for the training, a certificate to certify someone has completed the training, and activities to maintain that certificate. Brilliant! This concept has caught on big-time in government. Most jobs for government support by private companies require managers with a Project Management Profession (PMP) certification. I have mixed feelings about this. I think it is great that someone (or a group) is setting a quality standard for managers. But in a lot of cases, people are lazy and will opt for the easiest way out. I've seen experienced people who have a PMP (which means they passed a test) who don't know the first thing about management. If they do, they weren't implementing any of the PMI project management practices. How can this be? The answer is personal agendas and self-protection. These people can memorize facts for a test and pass. But it takes commitment to others and to the mission of the organization for which they work for someone to apply what s/he learned and practice it. It takes a lot of work. It takes emotional intelligence. Many managers have little or no respect for their employees and their needs. Their culture does not demand it.

Another outcome of an increasing population is that there are so many sick people. Heaven help you if you have to go the Emergency Room (ER) and need immediate attention. You have to wait for hours. During that time, you either die or prove that your ailment isn't going to kill you. It is depressing. My ninety-eight-year-old mother learned how to work around the system. She learned, from experience, that you get immediate attention if you go to ER in an ambulance. If someone drives you to the ER, you sit and wait for hours. One day my mother called me and told me that I needed to come to her apartment right away. I didn't question why and arrived. I thought she had a life-or-death situation. When I arrived, she told me to sit down. She explained to me that for several days she had had a pain in her side. She told me that it was so bad that day that she could barely walk. She told me that I was going to call 911 and get her an ambulance to take her to the ER. Then she proceeded to get dressed and get things together to go to the hospital, walking around her apartment. I called 911. When they asked me what the problem was, I told them that my mother was in such pain she could not walk. I lied for my ninety-eight-year-old mother. The ambulance came and took her to the ER, and the hospital gave her a bed immediately. They took her away to x-ray her lower body. After waiting a long time, the doctor came in and said that there was nothing wrong and that they were releasing her. I told her what the doctor said. She said, "What? Why did I come here then?" Which was what I was wondering. She then said that she felt better anyway because now she knew there was nothing wrong and that she would just have to deal with the pain.

There was a second time that my mother wanted to go to the ER. She had pain in her heart and stomach area. I told her this time that I would be taking her to the ER. Sure enough, we sat and waited and waited. She chastised me for not calling 911 for an ambulance and making her sit there for so long. This time it turned out to be gas. But her point proved to be correct. If you don't want to sit and wait for hours in the ER, call an ambulance. Otherwise, you wait among the many sick people in the waiting room. And, at times, there are so many of them.

By being a part of my mother's health care, I learned that there are so many sick people that there aren't enough people to take care of all of them in hospitals and rehabilitation centers. The last time my mother was in the hospital for a bleeding stomach ulcer (which bled for four days, requiring seven pints of blood), she basically lay in bed unattended for hours and hours. She received no special attention just because she was in a hospital. At the end of her life, during which she spent two months in a rehabilitation center, she also lay unattended for hours and hours. When she rang the help button and felt the urge to urinate or have a bowel movement, there were times she waited at least a half hour. A hundred-year-old woman just cannot hold an urge that long! So what good was it for her to ring? She learned just to fill her diaper and get changed twice a day at the scheduled times when attendants were supposed to visit her. Several times I had to tell the nurse on duty that my mother needed someone to look after her for a certain ailment. The nurse went to her room when she came on duty, looked at her and talked with her a couple minutes, then left. I guess if she was living, then she didn't have to worry. But when I spent long hours with my mother, I noticed things that weren't right and reported them to the nurse. Reluctantly, she investigated what I reported or called the doctor concerning what she then observed. I found that there were just not enough caretakers to care for all the people in the center. I found that everyone mechanically does what they are told is their job, but no one really thinks or has to think but the doctor. Yet the doctor does not have the complete picture of the patient like the attendants do who don't report anything. So how can the doctor perform at his/her best? It would seem to be a better system where all caregivers supported each other in total care of the patient. And then there is the administering of drugs that can do more harm than the ailment itself. Young people have trouble tolerating some of the strong meds they are prescribed by their doctors, let alone aged people! Doctors just experiment with drugs, trying this and that. But they are not present to witness the effects of the drugs they prescribe, which makes it more difficult for them to make necessary adjustments. My mother had some serious side effects from some of the medication she was prescribed. When I questioned the doctor, she told me that the drugs were necessary for the cure, and the side effects were secondary.

U.S. Politics

Jimmy Carter's book *Our Endangered Values* gives a bleak commentary on how politics are changing in the United States. He talks about how fundamentalism is having an increasing effect on politics and government and causing an increase in polarity of views. Republicans and Fundamentalists have linked up to push each other's agendas. We can see evidence of the polarity of U.S. politics in the work, or lack of work, of Congress. We can see evidence of fundamentalism in Congress's attempts to reduce women's rights—introducing bills to repeal abortion laws, eliminate funding to Planned Parenthood, and repeal Obamacare. These measures further the Republicans' cause of reducing government and government benefits to low-income people.

Politics in the United States are more and more influenced by capitalism in our country. The Republican Party strives to protect big businesses and reward those earning high salaries in those businesses. Their influence is causing the federal government and the middle class to shrink. There is more disparity between the wealthy and the poor. One thing that really bothers me is that getting elected to the presidency is directly proportional to the amount of money you raise. Money is the measure of success in politics. This severely limits the pool of eligible candidates. I would like to see people get elected who are qualified to run the country, not just rich, ambitious people.

I must say that the intensity of the mean-spirited things Republican politicians said about Hillary Clinton at the 2016 Republican National Convention (RNC) made me shudder. Some of the male politicians at the convention reminded me of a grade-schooler who gets carried away on the playground with name-calling directed to another grade-schooler and starts making up stuff for emphasis. These are grown men, however, not children, and they need to be held accountable by the public for their public behavior. Obviously, these men lack emotional intelligence and are not practicing its principles. There is no understanding there. They might as well be calling Hillary the B word, as so many businesswomen have been called historically for taking the reins and becoming visible leaders. The thing that was worrisome to me about the Republican Convention is that name-calling and discrediting a woman was done on public television and accepted by thousands of people. It was not only accepted, it was cheered! It was like a public stoning of a woman in Saudi Arabia. Never mind that she didn't commit the crime she was accused of; she is being used as an example. To me, this was a demonstration of sheep mentality. This mentality is counter to emotional intelligence.

The unfortunate thing is that Hillary Clinton's treatment at the 2016 RNC was only the beginning. I'm not going to even begin to address the political changes that have occurred since the 2016 election. Fundamentalism, as Jimmy Carter warned in his book *Our Endangered Values*, is undermining democracy and promoting authoritarianism. We must never take our democracy for granted. There will always be someone with a different viewpoint. Also, we must decide what qualifications we want our country's leadership to exhibit. How important is character and integrity? How important is leadership with emotional intelligence?

I'm familiar with the technique of publicly smearing others in an effort to divert attention from one's own inadequacies or incompetence in the workplace. I've had it happen to me, and I've seen it happen to others. It's called office politics. But here again, much of the time it is just plain lying. In order to promote his/her own agenda, a person starts saying negative things about another person who does not buy into his/her agenda. People believe what that person is saying because often that person is in a position of power or authority. So they should know what they are talking about, right? No one takes the time to check out the facts or to talk to the person being smeared to get his/her point of view. That is forbidden. And so the person with the agenda gets his/her way. This stigma follows that person wherever s/he goes since new managers often check in with previous managers before hiring someone.

I found that it is useless to run around and defend yourself to everyone who might have received the negative comments about you. And if you lower yourself to the level of the person saying negative things about you and start saying negative things about that person, you become the one condemned. People don't believe you. The saying is: "If you wrestle with a pig, you only get dirty, and the pig likes it." The best defense is to be the best you can be and go about your business. People will eventually see that the negative things either do not apply or have no relevance.

For a fact, there have been many times that I was chastised by my superiors for telling other stakeholders the truth. For example, when I first became a manager in a prominent federal government program, I went to my first managers' weekly meeting. At the meeting, the Program Manager went around the table for each manager to have a chance to report anything relevant to the program that he or the other managers should know. When it was my turn, I reported something to the Program Manager. After the meeting, both my bosses, the Division Chief, and the Deputy Program Manager cornered me and told me to *never* report anything at the managers' meetings. They didn't want the Program Manager knowing too much. I guess that was a test for me to see whose side I was on. I ignored their instructions and reported what I felt the Program Manager needed to know at those meetings. I failed the test and gradually fell out of favor with that one faction of the office.

What is scary is that the majority of voters in the United States have no clue how their government works. Since I spent my entire career supporting or working for the government, I tell people, "If people only knew…" Many times, politicians with no experience working in the government or with federal employees promise to make major changes and then take on a position (including the presidency) in which they are limited as to what they can do. They are accused of lying or being wishy-washy, changing their minds. Sometimes politicians *know* they are not going to be able to do what they promise, and they *are* lying. But sometimes politicians just do not understand the system. It seems to me, however, that more and more, politicians and persons in either senior executive service or political positions have no qualms about anticipating what someone wants to hear and then saying it. Many times, what they say has no resemblance to the truth or their intentions. To me, this is not politics; it is lying. But I guess that's because I am from the Show-Me state—Missouri. It took me a while to understand that, so often, people do not mean what they say. They just say what they think you want to hear.

As I discuss in the section on fear, Jimmy Carter, Al Gore, and Erich Fromm all describe how our politics today use fear to solicit supporters and gain control and influence of government policies. There once was a program on public radio on politics and immigration. The person being interviewed was an expert on immigration statistics. He reported that the influx of illegal immigrants was dramatically down. So, it was not a high-priority issue. The claim that immigrants are stealing jobs from Americans is also a myth. Immigrants from Mexico, for example, largely work in jobs that Americans will not take, like picking melons in hot, humid weather and other agricultural-type jobs. They migrate along with the maturation of crops that need harvesting. Other jobs immigrants fill are low-skill, low-income jobs such as landscaping. The interviewee claimed that immigration is commonly used to appeal to the older, white demographic who fear becoming a minority. The interviewee warned the public to beware of any politician who uses fear of any kind to secure your support.

On public radio the other day, there was a feature on immigration of Syrians into Germany. The previous year, Germans welcomed Syrian immigrants. The next year things changed. The press had been reporting terrorist acts in Europe by Muslim immigrants. The one attack in Germany, though, which the press was slow to report, was not by a Muslim terrorist but a German national. The press also started reporting crimes that implicated immigrants. But, here too, it was found that German nationals were more likely to commit crimes than immigrants. Now the German people don't believe what the press reports. They realized that politicians were using immigration to persuade people to support their personal agendas. It is no longer working because people check out the facts and use reason to form their opinions.

Education

For me and many others, education is important. For me, education provided independence and access to resources. A good education meant a better job and more money. Choosing the proper provider is important. Sometimes different schools or colleges are known for their quality more than others. At the college level, a quality school can be your ticket to immediate employment at the company of your choice when you graduate.

Students today are learning more, faster. Technology is aiding the education process. Students have access to an unlimited amount of information through the Internet. The old Britannia encyclopedias are a thing of the past. Just look things up on the Internet. Students can e-mail teachers questions, and teachers can e-mail students information, including reminders for tests and homework. Educational standards across the United States ensure that children in a certain grade can move to another location and be able to pick up and continue without more or less effort. There are always new methods of teaching, as in solving math problems.

Historically, the teaching profession has been taken for granted. Teachers received salaries lower than other professionals. Although they get the summer off, they have been required to work day and night during the school year, teaching during the day and preparing lesson plans and grading papers at night and on weekends. Often they are required to contribute resources such as utensils, books, and paper. My neighbor, who has taught pre-school and elementary school her entire career, said that it was nothing for her to spend $1,000 a year on teaching supplies, including pencils, construction paper, and glue. For a typical year, she had receipts for $5,000 worth of items she bought for the classroom. Although teachers' salaries have improved in recent years, they are still making personal contributions for teaching supplies.

With the increase in population, class sizes are often larger. This places more stress on both the teachers and the students. Since not all students learn in the same manner at the same rate, larger classes make it difficult for teachers to give individual students the attention they need. Often, teachers' aides have a cursory role and don't or can't delve into the special needs of a particular student. There are advantages of mainstreaming students with special needs. But, here again, if the classes are too large, an individual student may not be receiving the attention s/he needs.

The question for education today is what is the effect of students learning more, faster? And what effect is the use of technology having on children's social skills? If students are required to absorb and digest a certain amount of material in a certain amount of time, they have less time for social interactions and learning for fun. Sitting in front of a computer much of the day, they are not socializing with other students. During the 2020 pandemic, parents and child psychologists were concerned about children's social development and mental health when they were forced to be home-schooled. Education focuses on the capacity for the individual to learn, but is the individual training to be a robot? Having read three of Daniel Goleman's books on emotional intelligence, I am convinced that teaching emotional intelligence in grade schools is vital for the development of a child. But it is, as so many things are, a matter of the availability of funds. If there are more cases of maladjusted children bringing guns to school and killing fellow students and teachers, perhaps educators will realize that teaching emotional intelligence to their students might help them learn how to operate and cope in our society and how to deal with those who are troubled.

When you think about it, how can selecting one teaching method for all students be successful? A standard for all students is established, and then all teachers and students are tested against that standard. Although teachers, in their education and experience, learn how to teach students with different learning styles (e.g., auditory, visual, tactile, or kinesthetic), they find that they have to teach to the standard syllabus and the test on the material required for that point in the class. There have been several attempts to fix this flaw through Montessori schools and home schooling.

But for the majority of children, nothing has changed. And it is the education of masses that is precisely the problem.

I dropped out of a university post-graduate program because I was disgusted with the education system. I worked on my master's degree in atmospheric science when I was working for a federal office in the Midwest. My professional and school work were related; this facilitated getting my degree. After obtaining my master's degree, I decided to continue toward a Ph.D. I started by taking courses in statistics, since that subject intimidated me and I used it in my professional work. Shortly thereafter, I moved to the Washington D.C. area. My old office was planning to close due to government reorganization and budget changes. My chances of employment were higher in the new location. Once I started working in the new location, I enrolled at a local university in the School of Meteorology. I started with two courses in statistics. In one course, there were several teachers whose intent was to ensure the students learned all they could in the easiest manner. For the other course, however, the teacher was more interested in impressing his students with his knowledge and, in fact, made the material sound harder to the students than it really was. There were two big influences at work here. The teacher of the second course had his own agenda, which was different than that of the mission of education. His agenda was to make himself look better than he was. The reason for this personal agenda could be one of many things: he was insecure, he was bored, he was vying for a promotion or tenure, he needed to impress his colleagues, on and on. But it did not serve the mission of the students to learn and grow. The other thing I noticed about this course is that it was taught in the Education Department. That meant that the majority of students were female. In fact, in this class, there were only female students. Math and technical courses were not the focus in the Education Department. I, however, came from a very technical education in the meteorology area. During the teacher's lectures, I did not understand the material. But when I read the book, it seemed pretty straightforward and simple. I figured out that his lectures were intended to confuse the students and promote how intelligent and superior he was over his female students. Many were lost in the world of mathematical terms and logic. I concluded that the teacher had a personal agenda. After that realization, I paid no heed to his lectures and merely read the material in the book to obtain an A in the course. It angered me that the other female students had to struggle with the coursework because of a misguided teacher.

After the two statistics courses, I took a course in dynamics in the Meteorology School. I dropped that course for several reasons, one of which was because I was disgusted with the system. There was a professor assigned to teach that course, but he never came to class and never taught anything. Instead, for every class, a graduate student wrote gobbledygook (equations) on the board, facing away from the students. At the end of the class, after he had never talked to the students (only the blackboard), he assigned a number of questions at the end of the chapter in the book due the next class. I asked myself, "And this is teaching? This is our education system?" I was totally disgusted with this so-called teaching process. On top of that, the professor was never available to provide assistance with the material outside of class. The advisor I selected for my dissertation made no effort to be available to provide advice or counseling. That is when I dropped out of the program. I decided I did not need a Ph.D. to work in my profession. At the same time, I was traveling a lot for my job, so I made a choice—work or school—and I chose work.

I learned several things from this experience. First, this was another example of how the teacher makes a *big* difference in what you learn and how you perform. Good teachers ensure that their students learn; bad or mediocre teachers ensure that their own agenda is accomplished. Heaven help you if you get a teacher with his/her own agenda for a course; you most likely won't get the grade you could have gotten had you had a good teacher. Secondly, there is an arrogance in academia that does not serve it well and is detrimental to the students. It is a highly accepted practice for the professor of a course to do little to none of the work of teaching but to, instead, employ a lower-level associate to do the job. The professor can merely oversee the education of the students. (To their credit, though, graduate assistants can sometimes explain subject matter on a more understandable level than the professor, in better English!)

Other concerns in education are lack of funding in elementary schools and high schools. Programs are often cut or denied because of limited funds. These programs can be vital for a well-rounded education. Another concern is the bad influence on students from family practices, drugs, and peer pressure. A friend of mine who was a teacher, principal, and superintendent shared with me experiences at his high schools in lower-income areas. Much of his time was spent sending kids home who came to school drunk, breaking up fights among students, and talking to parents whose child misbehaved. Often times, a parent would threaten my friend if he tried to discipline his/her "baby." Without the support of parents, a school system's rules and discipline are meaningless.

And, of course, a concern now is that schools can be an opportunity for a terrorist to kill a large number of "the enemy." They can be a place where a disgruntled student can make himself or herself heard, to make a statement and declare his or her anger at others or the system. There was a feature on the evening news about Texas legalizing students in colleges to carry concealed guns. One student said he now felt safer carrying a gun to class. Is that sound reasoning? Are we fighting guns with guns? I am anxious to see how that plays out.

To become truly educated requires personal commitment and discipline. No one can instill those qualities in you. Scholarships can be an extremely important element of education by providing more people with the ability to go to college who otherwise would not be able to.

The Media

Today the media has a huge influence on what we know and what we think. So much of what we learn comes from movies and TV shows on streaming services. In early times of our nation, the public learned of important news from a town crier or bulletins; then telegraph and teletype; then telephone and radio; television; and now, instantaneously on the Internet using cell phones and computers. Television and radio have come a long way and are providing a wider range of programs these days. Television offers us talk shows, variety shows, reality shows, drama, documentaries and sitcoms. Television is a means to pay for and watch specially produced shows and movies on cable channels like HBO and Netflix. If you missed a regularly scheduled television program, no problem. You download it off the Internet. (Not like before where you had to record it on a tape or CD recorder with a timer). Television provides hourly and daily news. There are even cable networks that provide continuous news and sports. Public television and radio is a good way to learn, in more depth, about special people, places, books, and newsworthy events.

Evening television has evolved, too. Reality television has taken us into the daily lives of others and provided us with information we never really need. But it serves as a means for us to connect with other people in man-made or self-inflicted predicaments. The day after Sharon Osbourne found out that Ozzy was sleeping with his hairdresser, she did not appear on her daily talk show, *The View*. The next day, when she reappeared, she explained her experience and her feelings to the world. When Sharon and Ozzy started to talk and mend bridges, she explained on *The View* that she still loved Ozzy and that they had been together for thirty-six years. Then she said, "He is *still* a dog!"

Television evening sitcoms are, more and more, taking on relevant human issues. My friend Lauren said that growing up, she thought all white families were like the Cleavers on *Leave it to Beaver*. Sitcoms today, however, paint a more realistic picture of families and the issues they deal with. Does anyone remember when Ellen DeGeneres first "came out" on her sitcom? That was monumental for evening television. It seems so long ago and so trivial now. There are several sitcoms that I watched on a weekly basis because they are clever and deal with current human issues. For example, I loved the gay kid on *The Real O'Neals*. After he "came out" (on the first show of the first season), he struggled to find himself and other gay boys to relate to. Sometimes he had difficulty relating to his "manly" father and brother and bold sister. *Blackish* does a great job of dealing with issues black families and people in middle-class black families deal with on a day-to-day basis. I remember when the sitcom first started. I heard (white) people who had not watched it say that the show was racist. And I also liked *Last Man Standing*. One week's episode was about Mandy who wanted her father, Mike, to give a speech at her school so she would get extra points with the faculty. No one famous had accepted her invitation to speak. Mandy had a long list of things, though, that the school would not allow in speeches so that no one would be offended by a presenter's words. In a practice session, Mike started off, "Ladies and Gentlemen..." Mandy immediately told him he couldn't say that because some people don't identify with either. Mike continued saying that all you have to do is work hard and you will get ahead. Mandy told him that that wasn't acceptable either because some people work hard and never get ahead. Mike was exasperated. After a while, Mike tried a different approach. He decided he was going to speak his mind and never mind the school rules. He practiced his speech for his wife, Vanessa, and she told him, "There is no way you are giving that speech." The speech was full of "politically-incorrect" wording. Mike's next approach was to back out, much to Mandy's disappointment. She tried to reason with him that they were only words and all he had to do was write and give a short speech within all the school's limitations. He disagreed saying that he could not say something different than what he believed. He said he still believed in the American Dream and he himself was an example of working hard and getting ahead. He started with one outdoor store and now has twenty. He took Mandy to the site where a

Pakistani woman he knew had opened her first restaurant; now she has twelve. He made his point that entrepreneurs and pioneers did not worry about offending people. He said, "Do you think Elvis Presley was worried about who he offended?" The episode ended that Mike did not give the speech at the school that night; however, the Pakistani woman did. A concurrent plot was the lessons other daughter Eve learned when her best friend Cammy came home from college and she no longer needed Eve. And, of course, there is *Saturday Night Live*! It isn't a sitcom, but it *does* deal with relevant human issues. The cast's impressions of Trump, Hillary, and Sarah Palin are memorable and priceless. I've been watching that show since it first came on the air. When I was still at my parent's home and stayed up to watch it, my Mother attempted to watch it with me a couple times. I laughed continuously. She would say, "I don't get it. I fail to see what is so funny."

If we listen to the news on a daily basis, we will be left with the impression that the world is a mess. All we hear is one negative thing after the other. Most often, the daily local television news is an account of who shot whom, or who was found dead. I always think, *That is not news*. It is a report on "humans misbehaving." It's just an expected pattern of today's society. National news is scary, too. There is always some other country or culture who is out to get U.S. citizens. Our leaders are always trying to avoid confrontation or prevent violence that could affect the American people. At viewers' requests, national news has started reporting at least one happy human story each night, thank goodness. I refuse to watch television news at times because I choose not to be depressed and overwhelmed with information about sad things over which I have no control. Public radio has a better way of providing the news: it presents it in the form of education and in-depth information, though it is still depressing at times.

Social media helps you keep in touch with and share information with old friends, new friends, politicians, groups, neighborhoods, celebrities, and so on. It can be an awesome tool. Of course, it can be misused like anything else to hurt people. So caution and discretion need to be practiced when using it.

The media can make or break a person—a politician, an actor, a singer, a businessperson. If the media reports that a person is accused of a crime or bad deed, it is so easy for other people to condemn that person and assume s/he is guilty. That person could be doomed for life. In other cases, the reporting of a person's misbehavior can be excused or forgiven by many of the public and can influence the course of that person's life. For example, take the case of O. J. Simpson, a renowned football player. The media broadcasted live his police chase while in a white Ford Bronco in 1994 after the discovery of his dead wife and friend. This was one of the first broadcasts of this type and was an indication of how advanced live broadcasting had become. Now we learn of bad news within minutes of it actually occurring on the Internet, the radio, and on television.

The media has facilitated the rise of role models and heroes. Many of our role models are actors and sports figures. Why? Because they make big money and are able to live the ideal (in a capitalistic culture) of a rich person who does not long for anything (but a healthy, happy life). Many times the misdeeds of sports figures are reported to prove they, too, are human, even though they are making a huge amount of money and living lives of luxury. The media reports daily on the failed marriages and relationships of famous singers and actors. Once they rise to fame, their lives are public.

The media is capable of educating the public for the betterment of society. It can bring to light evil in the world in the form of discrimination, hatred, and misdeeds to society. It can emphasize the harm that misdeeds do to society and champion the high road as a solution. It has reported bullying in schools and the harm it does to students, including suicide. It has reported the discrimination that transgenders experience and the harm it causes them. Our local television station reports problems and resolutions that they facilitate for consumers that request their help. When I watched a television special on children choosing to identify themselves with their opposite gender, I was amazed. Children today are aware of their gender and sexuality at an early age and choose to be what they want to be.

One thing I learned as a practicing meteorologist is the shakiness of the accuracy of the press. Junior reporters would call the Weather Service and ask about weather forecasts or events. Many times I talked to the reporters myself. When I later read what the reporter wrote, I found at least several inaccuracies and misquotes of what I said. If there were reporting inaccuracies on things I knew about, how many inaccuracies were reported about things I did *not* know about? As a result, I am careful what I believe. This applies to all media, including the Internet. You can't be sure of anything unless you experience it yourself, and even then, there are doubts. It is a common joke that, if it is on the Internet, it must be true! One must realize that one must filter what the media offers. It is okay to turn off the evening news if you don't want to be depressed that night. It is okay to use caution when digesting the facts provided by the news or by the commercials in between.

Religion

Many of us grew up with the influence of one religion or another. Some of us had parents who practiced a certain religion and raised us accordingly. Some of us outgrew that religion as we left home and lived on our own.

The purpose of all religions is basically the same—to provide some moral rules or ethics for human behavior and interrelations and to provide means to feed the soul and spirit. Different religions have different founders or leaders (i.e., Christians follow the teachings of Jesus, Buddhists follow Buddha, Muslims follow Muhammad, etc.). All the leaders were prophets or forward thinkers for their time that influenced people. When you know and understand the commonality of all these religions, it does not seem reasonable to exclude or dislike people just because they belong to a different religion.

Growing up, a neighbor child was a good friend of mine. I was Catholic, and she was Protestant. One summer, she and I asked my mother if I could go to Bible school with her for a week during the summer. My mother said yes. I remember how great that made me feel. Here I was being asked by people in another religion to be and learn with them. I felt included and equal.

One thing I see with religion is that it can be limiting. It can be like an exclusive club. You have to do/believe certain things to belong. If you don't do or believe those things, you are excluded. Some religions even punish members in some way who act outside the rules.

It was very hard for me when I gave up the Catholic Church and stopped going to church every Sunday. This was a culture I grew up in and was comfortable in. I felt like an outcast and felt separate and different from my Catholic friends with whom I grew up. But there were several things about the Catholic Church that I could no longer accept as a reasoning adult. The disparity between priests and nuns bothered me. It bothered me that priests were viewed as mini-gods with freedom to own property and wealth while nuns in convents took vows of poverty and abided by strict rules of what they could and couldn't do. A man, of course, was at the head of the church and was viewed as infallible. Only men were allowed to lead or administer religious sacraments. A priest friend of mine said in jest, "Women have a place in the church; they clean it." Although it was supposed to be a joke, it so aptly described the traditional role of women in the church. I stopped practicing my Catholic religion long before priests' abuse of young boys and girls was exposed, having been covered up by (male) church officials. It was difficult to go against the culture in which I was raised, but my power to reason told me that I could no longer accept major principles of that culture.

The United States practices separation of church and state. I believe that this interjects an element of emotional intelligence into our government. It helps objectify government laws and regulations and removes emotional biases that many different religious sects could introduce. Countries where the government is run by sects of Islam rule by controlling its people's emotions—fear is used to ensure loyalty and obedience.

Jimmy Carter said in his book *Our Endangered Values*:

> "For generations, leaders within my own church and denomination had described themselves as "fundamentalists," claiming that they were clinging to the fundamental elements of our Baptist belief and resisting the pressures and influence of the modern world. This inclination to "cling to unchanging principles" is an understandable and benign aspect of religion, and a general attitude that I have shared during most of my life. I soon learned that there was a more intense form of fundamentalism, with some prevailing characteristics … To summarize, there are three words that characterize this brand of fundamentalism: rigidity, domination, and exclusion."

Not all religions are run by fundamentalists. But the fundamentalist movement is gaining numbers. The exclusion practiced by fundamentalists is causing a breakdown of communication that, in turn, results in hatred of others different than them. Fundamentalists are exerting more and more influence over our government and foreign policies.

The Times We Live In

We all know and have accepted that the year in which you are born has an influence on who you are or become. The terms Depression baby, baby boomer, Millenniums, and X-Generation are household terms and universally understood. Remember the hippy movement of the sixties? These terms represent certain personality characteristics. For example, the traits of miserliness and stoicism are attributed to people who grew up during the Depression. Baby boomers are known for the stage they are in. Right now, baby boomers are retiring and enjoying the good life, which is a product of their hard work during their career days. Millenniums are living at home with Mom and Dad as long as they can and are careful with their money since resources are more limited for them than they were for baby boomers.

Each decade is known for something different. In the sixties, it seemed like the young people were always demonstrating about something. Demonstrations were not as popular for a long time. However, they appear to have gained popularity again recently for various causes and movements, such as the Million Man March, Black Lives Matter, LGBTQ parades, and so on. Sometimes there have been riots due to perceived injustice. There have been sitcoms on television about families in the seventies and eighties. There have been technological advances each decade that helped shaped the young people of that decade. In the forties, people listened to the radio; in the fifties, television became the hot item; in the eighties, the Internet made its debut. The 2010s will likely be remembered for the iPhone and texting.

How often do we say, "Back in her day ..." or, "That's what they did back then." People growing up or living in certain decades believed certain things that changed with time. My ninety-eight-year-old mother, as progressive as she was, thought that doctors were all knowing, and she did whatever they told her until I called her attention to certain facts, such as the harmful side effects she had from drugs her internist prescribed her. She eventually started asking me to look things up on the Internet that she wanted to know about. I did and provided her printouts of information that was helpful to her. Also, my mother had never used a computer or any technical device. But when she was in her mid-nineties and losing her eyesight, she was determined to use a Kindle, which magnified the print of books she wanted to read. She had never used a toggle switch before, but she learned how to use one; she was that determined.

I am happy I grew up in the 1950s. I say that because it was a simpler time, not out of ignorance of social injustices that existed back then. Sure, we were all afraid of Communism and nuclear attack, but we weren't afraid of our neighbors. We ran around the neighborhood with our neighborhood friends up and down the street. We played outside all day and invented our toys. We grew up in an innocent time, unlike today when kids are exposed to evil human deeds on a daily basis. I remember, as a kid, Alfred Hitchcock was very popular. His productions were on television as well as in the movie theaters. My mother refused to let me see Alfred Hitchcock productions. She said they were too dark and, as a child, I did not need to be exposed to such darkness. Imagine that thinking today. No child could listen to the news with his/her parents; the movies and television shows they could watch would be severely limited. Yet, even today, I am glad for my mother's discretion. Even today, I do not like to see dark movies. I choose movies with a meaningful message and good human story.

Micro-cultures

The next layer underneath the U.S. culture is local culture. For example, the people I've met from New York have been fast-talkers and have fewer inhibitions than others from different locations. The people I've met from Texas have been very vocal about the fact that they are from Texas and think of Texas as one would a country they live in. I realize these are generalizations and may be less true as our society becomes more and more mobile. Nevertheless, they are examples of the effects of micro-cultures.

I grew up in the Midwest. Traits I associate with Midwesterners are honesty, loyalty, and integrity. Midwestern sayings that apply are: "I mean what I say and say what I mean" and "Show me" as in Missouri, the Show-Me state. I am seeing that there seems to be much more pressure in the D.C. area to be successful. Signs of success are owning McMansions and BMWs. There are social pressures and career pressures here that I never experienced when I lived in Missouri.

When I go back to visit in St. Louis, Missouri, where I grew up, I notice different things than I do in the D.C. area. One thing I notice is that, on the interstates there, people do the speed limit. I don't see people doing 30 mph over the speed limit, which is common in the D.C. area. Life is slower paced and more relaxed in Missouri. People are more conservative and politics is *not* the highest thing on their list of interests.

When my best friend from high school came to visit me, I used the expression "Everyone is a predator." Those words described my experiences in a highly-populated, highly-competitive D.C. metro area. It described my experiences here with bosses and the many times I experienced scams—telephone messages, e-mails, credit cards, hacking of government data bases, and more. My friend, in Columbus, Ohio, didn't have those experiences. In her career, she was a special education teacher and a teacher of English as a second language. She maintained close ties to the Dominican nuns who lived nearby and who did great things for the community. She had had a spiritual director for ten years. I agreed that her life's experiences were different from those I experienced living in the D.C. area. I have held many jobs and met up with many people with their own agendas. Since I did not have a support group like she had, I felt that I had to protect myself from people who had only their own interests at heart. This is not to say that I could not have created a support group for myself. We have nuns and spiritual people in Washington D.C., too. But the difference in our career paths did mean that, in my scientific career, I had fewer opportunities to meet the type of supportive, nurturing people that my best friend did in her teaching career.

Neighborhoods are also micro-cultures. For many years, I lived in a neighborhood known for its predominantly Jewish population. The temple was in walking distance. The neighborhood list-serve created a forum for people to help each other with contractor referrals and to share information about local government activities. My neighborhood in Silver Spring was much more formal than my neighborhood is now in Annapolis. The lawns in Silver Spring are all highly maintained. Many of the "lawns" in my Annapolis neighborhood consist of chickweed in the spring and crab grass in the summer. People also move to certain locations because of the public schools in the area. Montgomery County taxes are higher than those in Annapolis. The public schools in Montgomery County have a better reputation.

Family Influences

How many times do mothers get the blame for the neuroses of a child? How many times do you hear men say that their fathers left them or abused them as a child? How many times do you see children following in the paths of their parents and doing the same things, such as following the same career paths, adopting the same hobbies, or adopting the same bad habits such as smoking, gambling, and drinking? There is no escaping the fact that parents can make or break their children. Only the rare child can rise above parental abuse and suppress its effect so that s/he can grow to be a healthy, well-adjusted adult.

The first people to influence us are our parents. How they treat us as a baby and toddler determines a lot of how we view the world and ourselves. If they value you, you will value yourself. If they treat you like a burden, you will feel like a burden. Their view is your view until you start getting input from other people, as in siblings or other children and teachers in school. A sibling can counteract a negative parental view. For example, an older brother or sister who has already been through what you are going through can prepare you and shield you from your parents' negative behavior. A stronger-willed sibling at any level in the sibling lineup can help you to have a wider view outside that of your parents.

Remember the saying, "It takes a village to raise a child?" Well, that is no longer a normal practice in the States. More often today, a child under school age has a paid caretaker during the day while his/her parents are at work. That caretaker need not have any emotional connection to that child. His/her pay ensures that the caretaker provides the child the physical well-being the parents who are paying him/her are expecting. A caretaker is not expected to provide a child emotional care but can sometimes provide intellectual care, as in the reading of a book, expanding his environment, as in trips to the zoo, and so on. With the mobility of our society, families may move often and expose their children to several different environments during their lives. More and more often, people do not live in the same place that their parents or other relatives live. When children move away from their hometown and have their own children, grandparents are not readily available to help provide family stability and security along with emotional connection to their grandchildren. A sensitive child growing up without a sense of security in his/her own family can develop a feeling of loneliness and lack of self-confidence.

Both my father and grandmother influenced my choice to become a meteorologist—my father's love of science and my grandmother's love of nature. I told my mother, before my decision to become a meteorologist, that I wanted to join the United States Air Force and become a pilot. She told me that I wasn't going to do that; I didn't need that discipline. She was right; and, anyway, I don't think women were allowed to fly planes in the Air Force at that point, which is what I wanted to do. My father influenced my love of wood and refinishing it. My mother influenced my desire to decorate my house and make it a place of beauty. My father influenced my knowledge of and desire to maintain my houses. My mother taught me to have empathy for others and help them whenever I could. She taught me to be unselfish. Neither of them, though, tried to influence my education or career path. They left that up to me, which I appreciate to this day. When I found college very hard the first year and told my mother I didn't know if I wanted to continue, she said that I needed to make my choice. I chose to continue.

Children with stable and secure family lives with loving parents have a head start on life over their counterparts who come from dysfunctional families with abusive parents. Having loving parents gives children confidence; they feel loved and capable of doing anything. Loving parents teach their children things they need to know to survive in the unfriendly world. Children who come from dysfunctional families develop emotional issues that they have to overcome to find happiness and contentment.

Television and radio provide us with many stories about adopted children who look for and find their birth parents once they have grown. They usually come from happy homes with good parents, but that is not enough. These people have a need to know their heritage and need a sense of belonging to that heritage. Occasionally, the birth parents feel embarrassed or ashamed that they gave up their children for adoption. But the children are usually forgiving and understand the circumstances the parents experienced at the time of their birth.

Daniel Goleman quoted Dr. Frederick Goodwin, a past director of the National Institute of Mental Health, in his book *Working with Emotional Intelligence*: "There has been a tremendous erosion of the nuclear family—a doubling of the divorce rate, a drop in parents' time available to children, and an increase in mobility. You don't grow up knowing your extended family much anymore. The losses of these stable sources of self-identification mean a greater susceptibility to depression."

Influence of Friends and Acquaintances

All of us have stories of people who have come into our lives and helped us immensely or who provided direction just at the time we needed it. Some of us have stories about how we fell into a bad crowd and did things we later regretted. Some of us have stories about how one person saved us and then disappeared. As you go through life, your path will cross the paths of many other people. Some of those people will greatly influence your life.

My grandmother used to say, "People are like ships passing in the night." I had a hard time with this for a long time. I thought that all the friendships I developed should last a lifetime. It took me a long time to recover from losing a friend or friendship. Now I understand that I need to enjoy people and learn from them as much as I can while they are in my life because I could lose them at any time. By losing them, I mean they move, they stop wanting to be friends, they die, they retire to a different lifestyle, and so on. What is important is that we learn new things from each person we relate to. The things we learn widen our life's scope and enrich our lives by introducing new things and new ways of doing things that we would not have known or done otherwise. And each person teaches us more about human nature and different types of people doing different things. My friend Kurt introduced me to some amazing music. I've gone to some great live theatre shows because Donna wanted to go. I bought a condo in Florida, met some wonderful friends, and made money when I sold it all because Kurt's Mom lived in Florida and we used to visit her. I learned about some great TV series on Netflix and HBO and was able to watch them because Mary introduced them to me. I learned to modernize and minimalize my home décor from Sandy and Aggie. And on and on. And each of these friends is/was unique. I appreciate their uniqueness and their contribution to humanity.

Since we learn from our friends and our friends will influence our life's path, we best choose our friends carefully. By choosing, I mean continue to associate with people who can have a positive influence on us. I have found that my friendships just happened without my conscious will in the beginning. The people I met that made me think, *Wow. I would like to be friends with that person*, never seemed to be interested. When I would reach out to them, they did not respond. However, the people for whom I did not make that conscious choice to be friends but who exhibited qualities that I liked and related to seemed to choose me, and I signed up. There is truth to the saying, "Birds of a feather flock together." People, including managers, who did not share my values either stayed away from me or rejected me. As a result, all of my friends are people I either went to school with or worked with, except maybe a neighbor or two. They are people with whom I shared common values. Since retiring, I've made friends by doing things I enjoy on a regular basis, such as tennis, kayaking, walking and hiking, reading books and joining book clubs, and so on.

The key is to avoid those who use you to their advantage and at your expense and whose behavior does not allow you to be yourself and provide growth opportunities for you. In *A Road Less Traveled,* Scott Peck said, "Just say no" to harmful behavior from another. You have the right and the power to walk away from someone whose behavior you do not condone and which is harmful to you. It's okay to do that. I have done that many times in my life in both my private and work life. Sure you may have fewer friends as you grow older, but the friends that are left will be the people who enhance your life and well-being. You will be able to help each other accomplish your mutual goal of continual growth and improvement. I admire several of my friends today for the obstacles they had to overcome to get where they are. They are still learning and growing and are in their fifties and sixties, and seventies.

The Effects of Culture on Individuals

The result of the U.S. capitalistic culture is that people often live and work in fear: fear of being ostracized; fear of losing their jobs; fear of being alone; fear of not having access to resources they need to survive; fear of being harmed; fear of being found out (that they don't know what they are doing and live in fear). Alienation means that you are cut off from resources that others have to be happy and secure. For example, if a company or group of people ruins your reputation, you will have difficulty finding a job in the same company or discipline. Therefore, some people will sacrifice their integrity to keep in line and execute the wishes of their management, even though their demands may go against their principles. Others join the offensive and bully others to make sure they get what they want. They do anything they can to survive even if it means hurting others, lying, cheating, and so on. It takes a lot of courage to stand up for your own principles, to say no to unreasonable demands of management and risk alienation.

In recent years, I worked for a small government-support company. My supervisor in that company had been my supervisor in another company that we both worked for previously. When he had a position for me in his new company, he notified me. I joined his company in his open position. The longer I worked for him, though, I realized that he had psychological issues. I learned from my experiences and from the experiences of other women in the company, who related them to me, that he had underlying agendas. He confided in me when we worked together for the first company that he had an issue with women with power. I soon saw it myself. He asked numerous women to work for him and promised them great pay and promotions. But when they joined his company, he placed them in administrative-type positions with no promise of advancement. For a while, he let me work extra hours to get extra pay. I served in three different capacities, all requiring good management skills. But suddenly, I was no longer in favor, and he set out to destroy my career. I saw, though, that I wasn't the only person who was a victim of his disrespectful behavior. He managed to alienate everyone but a small circle of people in his office who, in order to protect their jobs, enabled his disrespectful behavior to others. Other contractors refused to work with him because he was so insulting and belligerent at times. He presented a favorable picture of himself to the president of the company who was located in Hampton, Virginia. I didn't know it, but he had designs to phase me out of my task and move two of his buds into the task. I was too costly. In other words, he could hire other younger, inexperienced men for less money. He was making deals with my government task manager who was a good friend of his. He convinced his friend that he needed researchers instead of a manager. His friend did not value management skills. So my boss secretly went about phasing me out. He had one of his flunkies send me an e-mail telling me that I was to work only half time on my task. Of course, the instructions in that e-mail raised a lot of questions for me, like, what was I supposed to do with the other half? I was told by the same flunky to ask my boss those questions. When my boss wasn't available to answer my questions (on purpose), I sent my customer an e-mail telling him that I would no longer be able to meet all his requirements since my boss was cutting my hours in half. I cc'd my task manager, my boss's friend. By his e-mail response, it was evident that my task manager was embarrassed that my customer had to find out this way. My boss was obviously misleading him. Not long after the e-mail exchange, my boss called me on the phone at ten at night to yell at me for talking to the customer. I was ready for him. I very deliberately stood up to him and calmly yelled back. I was hopping mad at the way he was communicating changes or not communicating them to the customer and me and let him know that in carefully chosen words. After we had both said our peace, he asked, "So where do we go from here? How do we get past this?" The short-term fix was that I would continue to work full-time on my task, but I was forbidden to talk to my customer. (Yes, I know that doesn't make sense). Next I was given a written reprimand with a fictitious account of our phone conversation. (He described himself as the victim). He and his flunky met with me to hand me the reprimand. I started reading it and realized what it was. It was my boss's way of protecting himself (fear) and making me look bad so that he would have a reason to get rid of me. I stopped reading it after I realized I was reading fiction, signed it (that I received and read it), and returned it to him. He said to me, "Is there anything in there you want to discuss?" knowing that there was no way I could agree with what he had written in the account. I looked at him and said deliberately, "You know how I feel." Then I picked up my stuff and said, "Off to the next meeting," and left. Within two months, he terminated me from the job. I saw it coming by then, though, especially when he asked to meet with me. He never wanted to meet with me. How did I react? The day after he terminated me, I felt like someone punched me in the gut. I took a photography job in the morning, but I felt sort of like I was floating through it, not totally there. When I got home, I felt sick. I vomited. I never vomit. It was like I was expelling all the evil and darkness I felt from that experience. After that, I could barely sit up. I lay down for a long while to recover. My neighbor brought me something to eat later that evening. By nightfall, I had recovered and resolved to find my next job and new adventure.

It is difficult to discern, in this example, whether this was a case of a man with a mental illness with unresolved anger and issues toward several different groups or types of people or a case of a man who saw an opportunity to be autonomous and take advantage of his positional power to accomplish personal goals of exerting authority. I know he had an issue with women in power because he told me so. He also complained to me about his wife (in his view) not appreciating him and complaining all the time about things he did or didn't do. This certainly is an example of the destruction to people's souls and organization missions that one person without emotional intelligence can exert if not held accountable. His ego was in charge and drove his actions. He lied much of the time. He made fun of people behind their backs, excluded others, and called people names. Since he was in charge, there was not much you could do to improve the environment he created. It was worst in the office where he worked, as related to me by a couple of the women there. When I encountered his misbehavior, I did what I knew was the right thing to do—reported him. But because he had the advantage of access to the president of the company and misrepresented our interactions, reporting him only made things worse. It gave him even more freedom to mistreat me. The only thing I could do was to leave the company. I didn't even have to make that move, however. He had already recognized that I could not support his misdeeds and exclusive, authoritative management style, so he terminated me.

Many times, managers are promoted and land in a position for which they are not skilled. As a result, they mismanage and make bad decisions. To show they are in a position of authority and can handle it, they behave in an authoritarian manner and do not take advantage of the knowledge and experience that their subordinates can provide. They impose their bad decisions on their subordinates with ill results: wasting money, poorer quality, resentment from their subordinates, and/or dissatisfaction from customers. Often, managers have their own personal agendas and find it necessary to step on their subordinates or suppress their knowledge to achieve what they want personally. They forego good practices that would execute the mission of the organization and raise the morale of the workforce. Sometimes the manager with his/her own personal agenda resorts to bullying the workforce in order to keep control and achieve his/her own goals. Sometimes a psychotic manager keeps changing the way things are done in the organization each day so that only s/he knows day-to-day what the score is, keeping control of the people in the organization and enabling the execution of his/her own agenda. The worker who interferes with this kind of manager's agenda is in for trouble.

I saw this happen while I worked at a large federal government bureau. It appeared that the government top management had a hard time finding candidates that best fit the position of CIO. The CIO I worked for when I first arrived at the office was an ambitious, self-absorbed man from private industry who was previously a managing director of customer service technology at a large, prominent company. His successor was hired (by working around the system) by the Bush administration. He had been a systems chief with the Texas state government. Probably due to their lack of experience in the federal government, these men resorted to authoritarian management practices and used the techniques I described above. Both were immensely disliked by their subordinates because of it. Just when we thought things were bad enough, they got worse under the second CIO. In addition to the authoritarian techniques used by the first CIO, the second

CIO rotated managers into different positions every couple months. As a result, no one knew what was going on or could manage or plan things. Chaos and discontent ensued.

I learned through the years that one is more likely to encounter managers with poor social skills and poor management skills in scientific, engineering, and IT organizations where the focus is on the technical rather than on people. I believe it is because these people are used to working by themselves and don't have to learn social skills early in their careers. When they are promoted to management positions, they resort to control and authoritarian methods partly because of ego issues and partly because they don't know how to relate well to subordinates. Also, these career paths tend to be male-dominated. So women have a harder time making it into management positions. If they do, they are often scrutinized more stringently and easily found with fault. I will never forget when, midcareer, I took a government-provided course with federal employees from different federal agencies. At lunchtime, I connected with a woman who worked for the Health and Human Services. I told her about the trouble I was having getting promoted or even just being treated fairly for the job I did. She told me she did not encounter such barriers or treatment. She was a GS-15 (the highest grade in that series of federal government civil service), and there were many other women managers in her organization. I was amazed. But, of course, she was in an agency whose focus was people's health.

When I read Adam Grant's *Think Again*, a lightbulb went on in my head. Scientists, he claims, are accustomed to "thinking again." Scientific research is constantly discovering and uncovering new information that necessitates reconsidering scientific conclusions. For the majority of my career, I worked in a scientific field. In college, I majored in science. But later in my career, I shifted to the Information Technology (IT) discipline. People who work in IT are used to deriving a final answer such as a software application, steps and final product of a project, and security tools to protect a network. Either their final product worked or it did not work. This could be one of the reasons why my scientific reasoning was not well received in the IT field. IT personnel were managed by authoritative managers who demanded final products on a schedule. I was used to rethinking the way we did things to improve work methods and procedures and, therefore, quality of so-called final products.

Life in the professional workplace has become more stressful. People fear for their jobs and safety. Many people who rise to the top do so because they have a personal agenda they are pushing (money, power, influence, etc.) and find a way to achieve their goals at the expense of others. But the price, sometimes, is great. Think about what depersonalization has done to our society. People feel like they are not acknowledged for who they are. Respect for one another decreases. People feel like no one is listening to them, that no one cares. People feel like they are invisible, that it's them against the world. Sometimes people do something or try to do something that sets them apart from their coworkers. Sometimes people become and stay angry for an extended period. Sometimes people resort to harming (even shooting) their managers and/or coworkers in extreme anger and loss of reason.

More and more, mediocrity is the name of the game. People who strive for excellence stick out from the masses and call attention to themselves. If a person chooses to work harder and smarter than his/her colleagues, likely one of the following will happen: the person's managers will feel threatened and punish the employee in one way or the other, or the other employees will feel threatened and undermine the employee to make themselves look better than the employee that is outshining and humiliating them. The person that sticks out soon realizes that s/he is going to have to make a choice: either comply with the unspoken culture or get out. I worked for a company once where I could not agree with the way they treated its employees or its customer and eventually resigned.

In the late 1990s and early 2000s, the big thing was "the best places to work." At the best places to work, employees were valued and empowered. Customer service was number one. Books like *Good to Great* described what companies did to get even better. It was usually hiring the right people, setting goals, and then empowering the people to accomplish the goals. I have worked for too many companies in more recent years that must never have heard about *Good to Great*. I see why they are called "Beltway Bandits." (There is a Beltway around Washington D.C. Most contractors that support the U.S. government do so inside or near the Beltway). Several companies I worked for had no intention of empowering their employees. In fact, many of their employees continually complained that they were "getting screwed." These companies did not hire the best people for the jobs, which did not serve the employees or the customer. Making money, even at the expense of good business practices, was number one. It baffles me how so many companies with poor service can continue to survive.

Punishment is dealt to people who don't comply with company culture. It is often more easily handed out to women than men since the men are usually in charge of the company and they feel women are there to serve them. (Hence their pay is less than the men's). Punishment can come in different forms ranging from removing job duties to termination. Men more often have each other's backs, and a woman is, many times, at a disadvantage to start with. Things have improved for women over the years, since women in the workplace are often not in the minority any longer. But more often than not, men are at the top making decisions for large organizations.

Capitalism does not provide for the feeding of one's soul unless one is able to work freely and fulfill his/her passion. Unions were established to ensure that workers' rights were not violated. Those rights were related to needs of the soul. Without unions stepping in for workers, companies could overstep their bounds in the name of production. For example, vacation time, during which a human worker can relax and regroup, is limited in the States. Too many and long vacations means less production. More work (pay) is required for more consumption (buying). Many offices are composed of standard-sized cubicles that make people feel like just another number. People tailor their uniform cubicles with pictures of family, plants, and posters to feed their soul and to express their personalities. In the government, if you experience discrimination or mistreatment, you can either report it to the Equal Employment Opportunity (EEO) Office or the Inspector General (IG). They may or may not be able to help you. There are some unions, also, for federal workers, depending on where you work.

Individualism promoted by capitalism means that people may feel less and less like they have a lasting support group. When people spend long hours commuting and working or are continually moving, they barely have time to get to know their neighbors. Sometimes it's our neighbors that are too busy to get to know us. It is not uncommon for children to move away from the location where they grew up, starting anew in a strange city. We get busy and grow apart from the people we held so dear growing up. As a person ages, unless he finds a supportive partner and a relationship that lasts, s/he can feel alone in the world. With this feeling of being alone in the world, you can see how, if something happens to you that affects you emotionally, it can seem more catastrophic than it really is.

My friend Mary, who I met through work, came from an unsupportive family of alcoholics. Her siblings profess to a different political viewpoint than she, so communication with them is limited and strained. She divorced her husband of sixteen years, who also was an alcoholic and a drug user/dealer and who beat her up on occasion. After she got divorced, she got a degree in computer science and moved to the Washington D.C. area to get a higher-paying job. One day, she called me to vent. She said the Republicans just passed a bill in the House that increased the age to sixty-seven for Medicare for people born after 1960 to match the age at which Social Security benefits would be available for the first time. Mary went ballistic. She was born in 1961. She ranted on and on to me for forty-five minutes about how there is no American dream anymore. The Republicans have taken it away. "I did everything you are supposed to do to get ahead and make something of myself, and the Republicans have screwed me and made it impossible for me to get ahead." The next day, I e-mailed her to see if she felt better. She then began the same rant in e-mails. I didn't see why this affected her so dramatically since she was going to have to work until sixty-seven anyway because of Social Security. But I realized that she has no one to turn to for help if she has little or no income when she reaches retirement age. She still has to pay off student loans, so she will never have enough money to buy a house. She just had had surgery on her neck, which ended years of pain. She was afraid that pain in the future would prevent her from working. She was in a panic. I can sort of relate to what caused her panic. I, too, have no one to turn to for help in old age. I have to make sure I have enough money to buy help when I need it. Mary started too late in life to accumulate any wealth to protect her in retirement. It was not her fault, but anything that reduces her income or benefits is a cause for panic for her.

In the medical profession, there are several things counteracting medical breakthroughs. There are several things causing more deaths and countering the population growth that medical breakthroughs allows. These things are disease, harmful drugs, and suicides. Disease can either be hereditary or environmentally induced, as in the case of cancer and heart disease, two major killers in the United States. We now know that persons exposed to carcinogenics greatly increase their risk of developing cancer. People who don't provide their bodies with the food it needs to fight off disease also increase their risks of developing cancer. Whereas, in the past, what carcinogenics are was either not known or suppressed due to capitalistic endeavors (such as, knowledge of black-lung disease could jeopardize the coal mining industry if more and more people refused to become coal miners), identification and acknowledgment of them are increasing. But we are realizing now that cancer and heart disease can be related to environmental stress as well as to other disease. Whole books have been devoted to this subject. Persons under mental stress of some kind can cause their bodies to react with illness of some kind, including migraines, shingles, mental illness, cancer, and heart disease.

The accepted practice is to treat illness with drugs. In some cases, drugs can be harmful and ultimately cause death, as in the case of mixing the wrong drugs, administering the wrong drugs, and overdoses. (Wrong here is used to describe drugs that are harmful for that particular person). Recently, there was a television news report on the increasing number of errors in hospitals where hospital staff administered drugs that either harmed or killed patients.

More and more people are using drugs to kill themselves either voluntarily or accidently. The suicide rate in the United States is on the increase. Drugs used to cope with life usually don't become one's friend. In many ways, when the body ingests something unnatural, the results can be harmful in one way or another, either with side effects or ultimate death.

As you can see from the discussion above, there are many things that influence a person's growth. None can take away from a person's true character, though, with which s/he was born and which s/he developed through childhood. They only build and add on to it. All of these influences are superficial things, and we more or less have some control over how they affect us. We need to know and understand the culture we live in and refuse to let any negatives we encounter limit us or bring us down. Sometimes we need to do things differently from those surrounding us. Sometimes it is best if we just move. Break the tradition. Go with your gut.

The next layer down speaks to the individual's makeup. Human beings are composed of the body, the mind, and the soul or spirit. All components must be in sync and serve the other for a human to be happy on this earth. When at least one part of a human is not nurtured, the human's equilibrium becomes unbalanced, and the other two are affected. For example, when one cannot or does not eat, the body becomes weak. It becomes harder to think clearly. It becomes impossible to do anything to feed the soul when the body is weak and the mind stops working.

Not until you understand society's influence on you can you understand what you can do to protect yourself and ensure that you develop a well-rounded, balanced, and educated view of the world and yourself. This view will enable you to keep growing and to find happiness and satisfaction with yourself and others. The downside is, if you grow as a person and stand firm in your convictions developed by experience and knowledge of human principles, then you can expect to be ostracized and even punished for standing out. You can expect to spend a lot of time alone. Some people find it hard to be alone. The key is that if you are happy and satisfied with yourself, you will be free of destructive emotions. If you don't want to be alone, you have to actively work at creating a support group of people that have the same values as you do. It is work. But you won't mind the work if you value yourself and want to do what is best for you.

Using emotional intelligence, we acknowledge the limitations placed on us by our culture and by society. Yet we rise above those limitations. We use our ability to reason to make the best decisions for ourselves in the light of who we are. We set out to influence others by our own example of love and compassion, for ourselves and others. As Marianne Williamson said in *Everyday Grace*, "Our task is not to avoid or deny the darkness in the world, but to lift it into the light."

In his book, *Man's Search for Meaning*, Viktor E. Frankl provides several insightful, hopeful messages for mankind. Frankl labored three years in four different concentration camps, including Auschwitz, during World War II. He was in his late thirties at the time and had been a practicing psychiatrist before he was imprisoned. During his imprisonment, he observed the behavior of fellow-prisoners and came to several conclusions. Frankl said that there were many people in the camps who turned against their fellow-man because they thought that was necessary for survival. But he said he could remember the men who "walked through the huts comforting others, giving away their last piece of bread." Because of this, Frankl said of these people: "They may have been few in number, but they offer sufficient proof that everything can be taken from a man but one thing: the last of the human freedoms—to choose one's attitude in any given set of circumstances, to choose one's own way." He said that every day presented opportunities to make choices—either refusing to submit to the powers that threatened to rob you of your inner freedom or allowing yourself to become molded into the typical inmate, renouncing your inner freedom and dignity. He presented the argument that these few men endured the worst of environments. They continuously experienced lack of sleep, insufficient food to sustain them, exposure to extreme weather conditions, and mental stress. And yet they were able to overcome those conditions to maintain their inner freedom and choose to help and support their fellow-man.

Another insight Frankl gained from his imprisonment was regarding suffering. He said that Dostoevsky's words came to mind: "There is only one thing I dread: not to be worthy of my sufferings." Frankl said that the way these few men bore suffering was "a genuine inner achievement." He said that they "bore witness to the fact that the last inner freedom cannot be lost." And of suffering, Frankl said: "If there is a meaning in life at all, then there must be a meaning in suffering. Suffering is an ineradicable part of life, even as fate and death. Without suffering and death, human life cannot be complete."

A third insight Frankl gained from his imprisonment and life's experiences is that "Freedom is only part of the story and half of the truth. Freedom is but the negative aspect of the whole phenomenon whose positive aspect is responsibleness." In other words, if man chooses freedom, he must also choose responsibility—to himself and to others. In summary, Frankl's message is:

> "A human being is not one among others: *things* determine each other, but *man* is ultimately self-determining...In the concentration camps,...in this living laboratory and on this testing ground, we

watched and witnessed some of our comrades behave like swine while others behaved like saints. Man has both potentialities within himself; which one is actualized depends on decisions but not on conditions."

Destructive Emotions/Behavior

I read the book *Destructive Emotions* by Daniel Goleman and the Dalai Lama. At the time, I was dealing with a mentally abusive partner and needed help. What I took away from the book is confirmation that I *was* witnessing destructive emotions. From that knowledge, I made my choice—to step away from them. The destructive emotions I talk about below were not chosen because of that book, however. They are based on my experiences and those emotions that are relevant to these times.

In his book *Our Endangered Values*, Jimmy Carter explained:

> "The revolutionary new political principles involve special favors for the powerful at the expense of others, abandonment of social justice, denigration of those who differ, failure to protect the environment, attempts to exclude those who refuse to conform, a tendency toward unilateral diplomatic action and away from international agreements, an excessive inclination toward conflict, and reliance on fear as a means of persuasion."

Pretty damning words! Do you also see these things?

We have all experienced someone exhibiting emotional immaturity:

- road rage
- bullying
- fits of anger
- name-calling
- refusal to cooperate
- undermining and blocking progress

- lying
- manipulation

These are examples of people lacking control of their emotions and pushing their own agendas. All my life I have struggled with the question, what do you do when someone directs this behavior toward you? I have tried many different ways to deal with emotional immaturity, and most of the time, I did not achieve the most desirable results—getting the person to stop the bad behavior. After years of experience, I would say that the best answer is to just say no to this behavior. But this is often easier said than done. Usually the perpetrator is persistent and does not let up until he/she does an adequate amount of damage to you. So, instead, I would recommend removing the emotionally immature person from your life. This may not be easy, but it must be done for your mental and emotional health. The bottom line is that you should take care of yourself.

I have read book after book, since I became a manager, to help me understand human behavior and human emotions. But nowhere did I learn how to deal with mean-spirited people who did whatever they could to further their agenda to look good and tear down the reputation of people who challenged them or who (unintentionally) made them look bad. I look back and realize that the same people who refused to cooperate with me and tried to ruin my reputation were just acting out of fear—fear of looking bad, fear of losing their job, fear of being disgraced, fear of losing their power, and so on. I would say that is what I learned from all the books I read about people's behavior. I realize that the same managers who did not support me in my work and instead tried to discredit me had managers themselves who did not support them and were behaving just like them.

I must point out that there are no wrong feelings. We can't help the way we feel. And we feel how we feel for a reason. But some emotions we feel can cause us to behave in a certain manner and can be destructive to ourselves and to others. For example, when I worked for a federal organization and constantly experienced bad managers causing harm to their subordinates' well-being and to the organization's mission and goals, I found myself in a constant state of anger. I constantly had to keep myself in check so that I did not react to the bad managers in a hurtful way and make things worse. I realized that this was not a healthy state for me to be in. The only way for me to change this situation was to leave that organization. So I did. Starting fresh in a new organization relieved me of the anger I felt toward incompetency in my previous organization. Had I not concluded that that was the best solution, I might have struck out at one of the managers, and s/he might not have understood. S/he most likely was unaware that my anger was just below the surface, ready to explode. S/he might then find it necessary to direct his/her energy to defend himself/herself and/or discredit me. Things only could get worse. Another example is that, in my previous organization, I found that the bad managers' insensitivity and careless behavior resulted in my feelings being hurt on occasion. Using emotional intelligence, I was able to understand the managers and the circumstances whereby my feelings were hurt. I was able to get past those feelings and move on to do my job appropriately. Had I not used emotional intelligence, I might be intent on retaliation and misdirected energy.

The sections that follow talk about emotions that can cause us to behave in a manner that is destructive to ourselves and others.

In my latter years as a government contractor, I put into practice "just say no." When I was a government employee and thought I could make everything right, I hung in there and tried to use reason and logic to present my case. After many years of seeing that approach fail, I resorted to just saying no. A recent example is when I was the communications manager on my company's contract to change a federal organization's e-mail system from various systems to Google in the cloud. After a while, a woman joined the transition team who was a federal employee but who had previously been a contractor. The team lead for the government was an insecure young guy who sought this woman's technical expertise. I had never in my entire career seen a woman so serious about getting her own way. Never once did I see her smile; instead she always had the sternest, scariest look on her face. I saw such darkness in her expression. At one point, the woman took it upon herself to decide that training sign-up should be automated—a different method than the training team had decided. She coerced a colleague to write software for a training sign-up system without the knowledge of the colleague's management or the knowledge of the rest of the team. At one of our regular team meetings, the woman triumphantly announced what she and her colleague had done. I was incredulous. The system had its advantages, but the fact that she had secretly completed the work, to me, was disrespectful to the rest of the team *and* her management. The disadvantage of the system was that there was a single point of failure. The developer had to be available at all times in case there was a failure (which there was the day it went live, and the developer was on vacation that day). The developer's management had not signed up to make sure the developer was either on call or had a backup during the training sign-up period. After the woman's announcement of her triumph, I pointed out to the Program Manager and the government team lead that taking a secret path that deviated from the team's decision was disrespectful to the rest of the team. But they did not support my view. That was just the beginning of her forcing her views on the team and the project. For me, the writing was on the wall. I saw that trying to deal with someone with no respect for her team members would only lead to disaster. I did not understand why no one called her on it. I think the company Program Manager was afraid of speaking up against a government employee. It was much easier to condemn me for speaking up, and it made him look like the good guy. So I asked to be relieved of my duties on the program. My boss agreed. After that, my company found a replacement for me. My replacement contacted me a couple times to ask me questions, but I recused myself. I didn't want to have a negative influence on her and the rest of the program. Learning more and more about what was happening, my replacement became exasperated at the poor manner in which the program was being managed and how one woman could cause such havoc. I saw that my choice to remove myself was the best choice. And I did it early enough so as not to create a division in the team—those for the coercive woman and those against.

Fear

I must preface this section with acknowledgment that fear as an emotion can be a good thing. It can be the result of a learned reaction to certain situations that might cause us harm. Fear causes us to avoid those situations or at least prepare for them and know what to do if they occur. Certain fears are necessary for our survival. But fear as an emotional basis for living life is destructive. Marianne Williamson said of fear in her book *Return to Love*:

> "Fear is our shared lovelessness, our individual and collective hells…When fear is expressed, we recognize it as anger, abuse, disease, pain, greed, addiction, selfishness, obsession, corruption, violence, and war…Fear is an illusion…Our fear is not our ultimate reality, and it does not replace the truth of who we really are. Our love, which is our real self, doesn't die, but merely goes underground."

My first real job as a manager in a large program taught me that many people work in fear, fear of losing their job. Yes, even federal employees who it is next to impossible to fire. If a manager gives an order, people execute it because they are afraid that they will be fired if they don't do what they are told. And in private industry, most likely they will be. In the federal government, there are things you can do to employees who "don't fit in," who question your orders. Most often they are assigned to "special projects," which usually are impossible to implement and go nowhere. This is the "kiss of death." What little respect you have for yourself is taken away. Everyone knows what this means. The results are the same as being fired. You are denied resources that others have access to and can bring you success.

For a number of years, I worked in a federal organization's modernization program to deploy Doppler radars. At one point in the delivery of radars in the production phase, the Deputy Program Manager (PM) decided to celebrate the production and delivery of the hundredth system. But he failed to tell the Program Manager. He picked a system site to start planning the celebration. But that site turned out *not* to be the hundredth delivery. Another system was delivered in between and was number one hundred. So what does the Deputy do? He rigs the contract delivery dates to suit his agenda. He could have declared the system he wanted as the hundredth delivery without falsifying legal documents. But he took matters into his own hands instead. I confronted him and my boss who supported him in rigging legal documents to serve unimportant minor agendas. My boss's response was, "Report me." He was challenging me to report him to the Inspector General (IG). I said, "I would hope that I wouldn't *have* to report you to the IG, that we could work out our differences ourselves." No response. Everyone in the office fell in line behind the powerful Deputy out of fear. You do not question him as I did. I think this is the point that I fell out of favor with the Deputy PM and his faithful followers. Although I was not afraid of being punished for standing up to the powerful Deputy like the other employees were, I understood why they were afraid. I forgave them for hiding behind managers who behaved unethically. I even forgave the managers who behaved unethically. Their underlying agenda, of which I was aware, was to impress the organization's top managers who were their customers and for whom they wanted to work when the program was completed. They were afraid that, after the program ended, they wouldn't have a job. I, on the other hand, would go wherever the government wanted and needed me to go. I was not afraid of going somewhere entirely new.

As a result, I had more compassion for government employees with misguided managers. But I found myself less and less tolerant of bad managers and constantly angry at their thoughtless behavior. I saw fearful people lining up behind the bullying, aggressive managers, condoning bad and sometimes unethical behavior, just to save their jobs. It became so obvious to me. I learned the hard way why people did that. I stood my ground and acted on my principles of honesty and responsibility. Because

I didn't comply with the bullies, I was the one that was ostracized. The bullies tried to discredit me and place doubt in the eyes of other top management regarding my solutions to program problems. The only way I could continue as a manager was to leave the program. It was a very sad day for me because I loved the program mission. But I was not willing to compromise my principles for the sake of one or two selfish, incompetent managers promoting their own personal agendas over the mission of the program. Only after I left did top federal organization management realize what I had accomplished and that I always had the mission of the program at heart. The Deputy PM was rejected by the federal management and retired; my boss was given a "special assignment" for ten years with no subordinates and at the service of another top manager.

One big fear I see in the workplace, besides fear of losing a job, is fear of conflict. People will do anything to avoid dealing with someone who has a different opinion than them. I am in the minority in the workplace because I believe that good comes from conflict. I find conflict brings two parties together to present different arguments, and good things result from learning and understanding each other's views. Win-win situations can result from conflict by melding ideas or by compromise. It is more frustrating to me when people avoid me without explaining the reason. I just wish they would be honest with me and tell me what is bothering them. Instead, I find people expressing their views to other people who either agree with them or who will not challenge them and not to the person who disagrees with them. Often, they undermine the person with whom they differ and try to discredit their view. To me, it would be much easier to come together and work it out. Some people put a lot of energy into thinking of ways to discredit their opponents. This energy could well be put to better use to collaborate on a solution together.

My elderly neighbor across the street asked me whom I was going to vote for in the 2016 election. When I told him, he said sincerely, "Oh, that's bad news. I'm sorry to hear that." Next time I saw him, I said something about working on my house. He said, "You better enjoy it now because if Hillary gets in, she is going to take it away." Clearly there was no deductive reasoning that backed that comment. I responded, "Did you hear that somewhere or are you just making that stuff up?" He didn't respond to that and changed the subject. Did he actually think he was going to scare me?

My best friend from high school related the following story to me. She was a special education teacher and also taught music therapy and English as a second language in Columbus, Ohio.

"For many years (at least twenty), schools have included conflict resolution in their curricula. Kids are trained in active listening techniques and asked to volunteer as moderators in actual conflict situations. For example, two students who had been fighting at school were required to meet with each other in the presence of a student moderator and a teacher or guidance counselor. The two fighters each stated their case and their feelings and were asked by the moderator to restate what the other person said to assure him he was heard (active listening techniques). This kind of communication went back and forth until a better understanding (of feelings and reason for the behavior) was reached, and then a game plan was discussed. The student moderator guided the process, and the classroom teacher or guidance counselor stepped in *only* if the process was breaking down. It worked incredibly well, even at the elementary level. I watched this procedure when two third graders (one from Iran, whose English was very limited, and the other American) were constantly fighting on the playground. After back and forth statements, the truth finally came out. The American kid said, 'My mom says that you're Muslim and I'm Jewish, and we're *supposed* to hate each other.' It ended up with the teacher having a conference with the mother, and the fighting finally stopped. It was a learning experience for the kids and the mother, as well as for the teacher!"

On public radio, there was a feature on what a Danish town did when they realized that many of their young male Muslim immigrants were leaving for Syria to join ISIS. They interviewed both a young Somali immigrant and a town official. The Somali immigrant explained that he belonged to the only black family in the neighborhood. He got into a situation at school when the students were asked by the teacher to discuss Islam. A white girl made it personal against Jamal and said that because he was Muslim, he was a potential threat to Christians and was dangerous. Somehow, what she said escalated, and the police got involved. They went to his home and searched the house, humiliating the family. Shortly after that, his mother died of a heart attack. Jamal blamed the citizens of the town for her death. He was angry. He said, "If they labeled me as a terrorist, that's what I'll give them." He prepared to leave the country for Syria to join ISIS. Meanwhile, the leaders of the town were searching for a resolution to the fact that every day, sons of immigrant Somalis were leaving town for Syria. Their families were distraught. The town's people decided to change their approach. Instead of exhibiting fear of these potential terrorists, they decided to embrace and support them. They developed a program whereby they supported young immigrant Muslims and provided them opportunities for education and open communication. They folded them into the community. The town leaders approached Jamal before he could leave for Syria. One of them called him and said he was sorry for the way Jamal had been treated by the community and invited him to come talk with him at a coffee shop. His apology completely turned around Jamal's view of the town. He accepted the invitation and eventually became integrated into the community. There were a couple young men who returned to the town from Syria. They expected to be incarcerated. Instead, the town leaders welcomed them back and invited them to participate in the program they had established for young immigrants. One young man had been injured while he was away. The program leaders asked him about his injury. The young man replied that he had been in an accident, denying that he had fought for ISIS. (It was illegal in Denmark to fight for terrorist organizations). Although the program leaders believed he had been injured in fighting, they accepted his explanation and included him in the community program. They showed him that they trusted him. As a result, there have been fewer Muslim immigrants leaving the town for Syria. It turned out that these young men desperately wanted to belong and were angry about the way they were rejected by the town's people. When the town included them and treated them as equal human beings without fearing them, the young men reacted in turn. They chose to stay and become respectable citizens of the town.

This is a great example of how fear can break down communication from both sides. It is an example of how exclusion causes anger and creates enemies. Inclusion and openness turned things around in that Danish community. So, I would say, using emotional intelligence tells us that blowing up and killing radical Muslims is not going to cut it. Are we going to wipe out thousands of people? That is genocide, isn't it? Only it is right because the United States is doing it? The emotionally intelligent way to fight radical Islam is by teaching and spreading an alternative philosophy that more people will welcome, just as we did with communism. The Chinese who embraced communism are now embracing capitalism (for better or worse).

My best friend from high school told me that where she teaches, multicultural festivals are held at elementary, middle, and high school levels. The festivals are designed to include refugee and immigrant students. In February, there is emphasis on African American history and African American students. The middle school history curriculum includes the history of the major world religions and how they influence the culture of the time as well as modern culture. All of these things are building blocks for emotional intelligence for young people. Of course, there were parents who didn't like these things being included in the education of their children. But emotional intelligence tells us that the children's education in these areas is about the facts, not about persuasion toward one culture/religion.

Teaching and spreading emotional intelligence shows people how they can control their emotions and act upon reasoning and understanding. No more aggression, no more fear, no more suppression. In his book *Our Endangered Values*, Jimmy Carter put it this way: "I am convinced that our great nation could realize all reasonable dreams of global influence if we properly utilized the advantageous values of our religious faith and historic ideals of peace, economic and political freedom, democracy, and human rights."

I watched a program on public television called *Saudi Arabia Uncovered*. It was really scary to me, and I can't stop thinking about it. It consisted of videos that undercover Saudis snuck out to the United States to expose how life really is in Saudi Arabia. The videos were very graphic. Basically, the Saudi Arabian government is using fear to manage its population.

Anyone who speaks out against the government and its religious rules is publicly lashed, beaten, imprisoned, and/or beheaded. Beheaded bodies are displayed in public places. There are teams of "moral police" in white robes who monitor people's behavior and retaliate against them if they break the rules. In one segment, the photographer showed a video of himself playing a guitar in an open space. The video showed the moral police approaching and then went blurred. He later recorded an account of what happened. The police smashed his guitar and broke his finger. Playing music is not allowed in Saudi Arabia. It is a sign of evil and the devil. Other videos showed men slugging women in public places. One video did show the moral police catching up with a man who slugged a woman in a grocery store and arresting him. Another video showed a woman accused of molesting her own daughter, her head covered in a black bag, being wrestled to the ground in a public place, and her crying out, "I didn't do it!" They beheaded her and then displayed her beheaded body. Another video showed a child reading a textbook, and the commentary told what the text said in English. The textbook said that Christians and Jews were to be hated and killed. This is what radical Islam is teaching young children in schools.

Many things concerned me about the content of this program. First, the Saudi royal family advertises how rich the country is while, in actuality, it is only the royal family and not the general population. Begging is common in the country, and the lower price of oil lately lessened benefits the government was providing the poor. Second, Saudi Arabia is an ally of the United States. Is that on false pretenses? Is it because Saudi Arabia is claiming to be something they are not? Are we allies with a country that suppresses its people and instills fear in them to comply with obsolete religious beliefs? Are we allies with a country that kills its own people if they express things that come from the soul? Third, the teaching of hatred and fighting of people of different religions to children is another method of brainwashing the entire next generation. The hatred and killing will continue for generations to come. If this is what is happening in Saudi Arabia, there are many other countries in the Middle East where Islam is the religion of the majority that are most likely behaving in the same manner.

I can't see the difference between life in Saudi Arabia and life in Hitler's Germany or in communist Russia. People who think differently than the ruling government are beaten or annihilated. People live in fear of their lives every day. People upholding the ruling government are warring against other countries. Like communism, radical Islam is a philosophy of living. Islam is a religion, but I argue that radical Islam is not a religion. It is using the name of religion to endorse itself. It is a philosophy of ruling through emotional control.

To me, this is the opposite of emotional intelligence. First, people are acting out of emotion only, without reasoning. People are acting either on aggression or fear. The aggressors instill fear in the suppressed. They bully others into doing or not doing whatever they decide. People are not allowed to think or reason on their own. They are only allowed to act on a strict set of religious rules chosen by the government. It isn't even enough that they do this to their own people. The radicals are extending their acts of terror to other countries to instill fear in people of other religions and philosophies. And it is working! Fear is spreading and causing us to make choices for ourselves that we would not otherwise make.

What is bothersome is that here in the United States we have the freedom to think and reason. Yet, because of some words instilling fear in us by politicians or our own lack of knowledge of the facts, we are not using reason to make sound decisions for ourselves and our country. The easy way is to follow like sheep tricky politicians to the edge of the cliff. Hopefully, our nation will come to its senses before falling off the cliff.

In his book *Assault on Reason*, Al Gore said:

> "Fear is the most powerful enemy of reason. Both fear and reason are essential to human survival, but the relationship between them is unbalanced. Reason may sometimes dissipate fear, but fear frequently shuts down reason. As Edmund Burke wrote in England twenty years before the American Revolution, 'No passion so effectually robs the mind of all its powers of acting and reasoning as fear.'"

Hatred

In *Everyday Grace*, Marianne Williamson said:

> There is so much love in the human heart, yet hatred
> threatens our planet. And why? Because hatred is currently
> more committed than love. In the words of philosopher
> Edmund Burke, "The only thing necessary for evil to
> triumph is for enough good men to do nothing." Indeed,
> the forces of fear in this world are more disciplined, more
> courageous in a perverse kind of way, than are the forces of
> love. For hatred, as we know all too well, has no problem
> announcing itself and its intentions to the world.

Every day on the news, we hear stories of hatred. Terrorists have bombed
large numbers of people of a different religion or way of life in a public
gathering. A mass shooter shoots large numbers of people and then
commits suicide. A cop is killed just because he is a cop. A gay person is
refused service in a restaurant. This is our news today. These are examples
of deliberate, visible acts of hatred. None of them are acceptable, but we
are becoming conditioned to the fact that this is the world we live in.

Other acts of hatred are less advertised but are, nonetheless, as
debilitating. Denying someone his/her rights to a job, a home, service, or
anything else just because of his/her race, gender, age, or sexuality is an
act of hatred. It is against the law. Yet we see examples of discrimination
all the time.

Another sign that hatred is becoming accepted in our daily life is in U.S.
politics. The 2016 Republican presidential campaign is unprecedented.
Never before in the history of the United States has outward hatred and

inciting rhetoric been so openly expressed. Banners were waved at the Republican National Convention that said "Lock her up." On August 15, 2016, the *Washington Post* carried an article about retired Lt. Gen. Michael T. Flynn saying he "has cast the presidential race as a continuation of the career he spent battling dangerous enemies in distant wars." The *Post* quoted Flynn at a rally in the state of Florida where he said, "The enemy camp in this case is Hillary Rodham Clinton…She is somebody who will leave Americans behind on the battlefield," while the rally attendees held up banners saying "Lock her up." Rhetoric of this type condones and promotes hatred. When either candidate is finally elected, they will have to get past the emotions of hatred aroused during the campaign to work with a bipartisan Congress for the betterment of the nation. But as we saw, this did not happen. Hatred was the theme of a four-year administration.

It is hard not to cringe at the acts of hatred committed in our country in the name of patriotism. It is hard not to hate a person or group of people who intentionally act out their hatred of us. But the only answer is to keep exhibiting love. Thank goodness the Democrats did not respond to Republican hatred in the 2016 campaign with more hatred and inciting chants. Hatred stops with us. When we are committed to love as much as people are committed to hatred, we can stamp out the destructive emotion of hatred. We can accept that it will always be there somewhere, but we will not let it rule our actions.

As a woman in a predominantly male career field, I experienced many cases of discrimination. Very early in my career, I was promoted to the position of Disaster Preparedness Meteorologist (DPM). This happened only because the man next in line to get it took a job out of town. The Central Region Director visited our office shortly after I was appointed. He said to me, "I only hope you can do as good a job as Dick did." Dick was the previous incumbent who ran two businesses from the office and who sat with his feet up on the desk and listened to music when he was on "extra shifts." *Yes*, I thought, *I believe I can*. I will never forget that condescending remark. At the time, I just smiled and agreed. I once applied for a job in Central Region Headquarters. Shortly after I submitted my application, I visited headquarters for business and stopped by to visit the hiring manager. He could not look me in the eyes and looked elsewhere when I asked him a question. He danced around his office nervously and sort of inched me out of there as fast as he could. Needless to say, I did not get the job. There were no women managers in Central Region Headquarters at that time. After I had been in the DPM position for a while, the Meteorologist-In-Charge (MIC) would plan trips for both of us to speak to various disaster preparedness groups. At the last minute, he would consistently cancel, and I had to go by myself. None of the men traveled by themselves; they always had a companion. But I always traveled by myself for my DPM job. At one point, I got up enough courage to ask the MIC why he always promised to travel with me then canceled at the last minute. He responded, "Because my wife doesn't like it." As hard as I tried to believe that, I just couldn't. Although I was saddened at the discrimination I experienced, I never let it discourage me from doing my job and doing it well. I was determined to be the best I could be at whatever I did.

Hatred is like a cancer. It eats at you until something bad happens: you explode and say things you shouldn't and get fired or end a relationship; you shoot someone and go to jail the rest of your life; or you get physically ill and suffer much pain. The most common consequence is that you yourself become the victim of acts of hatred. We all know that we reap what we sow. What happened on January 6, 2021, at our nation's Capitol was the ultimate act of hatred. There were injuries and deaths. Individuals who led, participated in, or enabled the attack are being held accountable. A large number of people were arrested and charged with crimes.

Anger

Earlier I provided Daniel Goleman's quote defining emotional intelligence. He said emotional intelligence is: "As Aristotle put it, the rare skill 'to be angry with the right person, to the right degree, at the right time, for the right purpose, and in the right way.'" Anger in itself is not a bad thing. Anger is only bad when we allow it to linger and cause us to behave in a hurtful manner. Emotional intelligence tells us when and how much anger is okay. Emotional intelligence tells us how to express it appropriately. Recognizing our anger is the first step. It is necessary to admit we are angry before we can do something about it.

Anger can be like a cancer and can even cause cancer. Goleman calls anger the "emotional cousin of hatred and resentment." I've heard stories about people who did spiteful things to others out of anger. Anger can eat at you mentally and physically until you are depressed and ill. So many of the lone wolf shooters we hear about in the news are angry loners who allow ego and anger to take over until they ruin their lives and the lives of many others.

Daniel Goleman said in his book *Destructive Emotions*: "Buddhists strive to be totally free from anger, while most Westerners view anger, in the proper degree and situation, as perfectly suitable—and few consider whether we can eradicate it altogether."

Hurt and anger are emotions that come suddenly like a wave over us when something triggers them. We have a tendency to lash out at the source of our hurt and anger. But that usually is not productive, nor does it result in positive solutions. It is best to cool down and think about what happened and what the best course of action would be.

When I was a CIO in the Office of the Secretary of a federal agency, occasionally one of my employees would do something that I viewed as either stupid or bad for our customers. One time, and one time only, I displayed my anger and told one of my employees that what he did was wrong. In his defense, the employee explained why he did what he did. His explanation made sense to me. From then on, when someone did something I didn't agree with, I first asked them, "Why did you do so and so?" Their explanation usually made me feel better about what had happened. I then explained to them that, in the future, there was an alternative way of doing things and asked that they consider doing that instead. That one experience taught me never to be quick to judge someone without knowing the facts about what they did and why. The best way to learn those things is to communicate openly with the person.

On a personal level, I try to do the same thing. If someone hurts my feelings, I first ask them, "Why did you do (or say) so and so?" I try to understand where they were coming from with their explanation. After they explain, I tell them, "When you did (or said) so and so, I felt so and so." That gives the other person a chance to understand how his/her behavior made you feel and to think about a way to avoid the behavior in the future. Hopefully, they will say they are sorry to let you know they are remorseful that they hurt your feelings.

In some cases, I have lost "friends" who suddenly just stopped communicating with me. It bothered me and I kept asking myself what I did to drive them away. In my mind, my friends are friends for life and I have a certain responsibility to them. However, not everyone thinks that way. People change somewhat as they age. When they discover that a "friend" is headed in a different direction than they, they may feel they owe nothing to that person and prefer to avoid having to confront them with the truth about how they feel. They then cut off communication to avoid having to explain. As my grandmother told me, "People are like ships passing in the night."

Letting your emotions get out of control and saying hurtful things to the other person only breaks down communication. Both of you are then hurt and unwilling to communicate.

Always think about how you can objectify behavior. Think of the behavior as separate from the person. This will prevent you from personalizing your reaction to hurtful behavior and calling the other person names. Make sure the other person understands what happened and takes responsibility for hurting you. If s/he does not and is a repeat offender, then you have to ask yourself the value of the relationship. Is this person hurting you more than s/he is supporting you to be the best you can be?

I've had intimate relationships with three men (two of them were my husbands) and a friendship with one woman that did not last a lifetime because their behavior indicated that they did not value our relationship. I saw that their own agendas were usually more important to them at the expense of our relationship and collective agenda. This view caused numerous occasions for hurtful feelings by me until something eventually happened that caused me to say, "No more." I do take responsibility for letting these people into my life and sticking with the relationship as long as I did. I made the choice to keep changing my behavior to accommodate them until I finally drew the line. The way I look at it, I had a choice: either discontinue seeing them immediately once I realized that we had different principles, or keep enjoying what we shared together and the good times. There are too few people just like us to refuse to associate with someone for fear of the friendship eventually ending. I believe that there is a normal flow of people into and out of our lives. We come together when there is a mutual need, we help each other out, and then we move on. This, of course, would explain why there is so much divorce in our country. With lasting marriages, however, two people who are well suited for each other work out differences and commit to their relationship over and over again.

Mental or Physical Abuse

If someone abuses you physically, that is a no-brainer. You should not allow that to happen again. You should immediately walk out of the life of a repeat offender. Of course, this requires courage and hard work. And you must protect yourself in the future from physical abusers since we often repeat patterns in our lives, including selecting the same type of partners. I have friends who had husbands who beat them up. Leaving them was the hardest thing they had to do in their lives. But they did what they had to do. They eventually pieced their lives back together and were the better for it.

A mental abuser is a more elusive matter. I had a mentally abusive partner for seven years. I don't think he meant to be abusive, but I believe his behavior was consistent with his role model, his father, who was abusive. And the abuse was not continual or even the majority of time. I always believed that I could tolerate it and ignore the bad times for the sake of the good times. But, believe me, you will not conquer mental abuse alone. If you are unable to get the abuser to see what s/he is doing or to see a therapist who can help him/her to recognize how his/her behavior is abusing you, you need to walk out of their life. If you don't, you are only postponing the inevitable at your own expense. No person should make you feel less of a person than you are. No person should inflict restrictive rules on you that limit your growth as a person. This person can destroy your life and your health if you let them.

In my case, I just became hardened to my partner's behavior. I kept adjusting my own behavior and mind-set. I allowed his abusive words or behavior to affect me less and less. I grew less and less surprised and tolerant of his angry outbursts and drama sessions. I trusted and respected him less and less. What my partner *did* recognize was the change in *my* behavior. When he no longer felt revered by me, he decided to move on to find someone else that would revere him. I was devastated. I had loved him enough to put up with his antics for seven years, and then he moves on to find someone else to love. The first time I saw him with another woman, it felt like a knife went through my heart. It took me a year to get over it. But eventually I let reason overtake my emotions. I reasoned that breaking up was the best thing for both of us. We had both learned a lot from each other, but we both needed something else that we couldn't provide each other.

Kurt and I have remained friends for the past fifteen years. Kurt has usually been in some kind of relationship with a woman during that time, each lasting about a year. Kurt invites me to get together in between those "relationships." Kurt has recently warned his "new women" about our friendship, which he claims will continue during his new relationships. Kurt is now always pleasant to me. We have no expectations from one another. He seemed to just want the freedom to do whatever he wanted. I see he has grown and learned a lot from the other women with whom he has had relationships. I think he now values what he had/have. We still respect each other for who they are. I realize that this type of friendship is rare; I have had no communication with my two husbands whom I have not seen since we split.

One time a mutual friend of mine and Kurt's, with whom I had a seven-year relationship, said to me, "How can you still talk to him after the way he treated you?" I think she felt protective of me as a fellow professional woman. Her question made me think. I came to the realization that I felt that Kurt was Kurt and would always be Kurt. It was I who chose to stay with him and kept adjusting my behavior to keep peace and keep us together. I could have left the relationship at any time and said no to the abuse, which I eventually did when my "limit" was reached.

We hear on the news more often lately how some athletic icon or law officer was abusive to his spouse. My own mother had a friend who was married to a policeman. She suspected that he abused her physically on occasion. But her friend would never talk about it. These appear to be cases where the ego is in control. When people are in positions of power or authority in their work, it is hard to separate the stream of consciousness you have at work from that when you go home. At work, you have to take charge and be aggressive. Then you go home and you have to be sensitive and caring.

And there is abuse in the workplace. It is usually in the form of an abusive boss that causes a high level of stress. Sometimes we find ourselves in jobs that have continual short-term deadlines and bosses who take advantage of our skills and knowledge. Because we take responsibility and get things done, our reward is more things to do and deadlines in which to get them done. This happens over a course of time until, sometimes, we find ourselves stressed by what we have yet to do and a boss's continual oversight to see that we have met deadlines. My body usually tells me right away if I am stressed. I get a tightness in my chest. When I get that, I step back and try to fully understand what is causing it. I then set about changing something that needs to be changed to rid myself of the symptom.

I lost a dear friend, and I blame her abusive managers, at least in part, for her death. Logically I know that it was her destiny, her makeup, and probably her inherited genes that caused her to die young at the age of fifty-one of a heart attack. But I witnessed the stress she was experiencing at the time of her death. In fact, I talked to her the evening before she died. She told me, "If I could, I would just put everything (her work) on my chair (at work) and just walk away." She felt trapped. Her only escape was to leave this earth. The Director of her office took advantage of her caring, conscientious, responsible work habits. He and a man in the Contracting Office worked her into the ground with continual demands and deadlines. She could never catch up with their expectations of her. The Director could have gotten her help but did not care to pay attention to what was happening to her. He had his own problems. Sarah worked long hours during the week and on weekends. The last time I visited her, she was in her office with her back to me as I walked in. I said, "Sarah?" When I saw her face when she turned around, I was taken aback. Her face said it all. She was stressed to the max. It scared me. We were supposed to have lunch that day, but she asked if she could postpone due to another imposed deadline. We never got to have lunch before she died.

And work was not Sarah's only stress. She had neighbors on the one side of their house who were "off the deep end." They were both federal employees who supposedly worked from home. But, from what the neighbors could see, they did not spend the entire day at home inside on their telework days. These neighbors took on a vendetta against Sarah and her husband. Their behavior was just plain harassment. They put up security cameras that were pointed at and filmed everything Sarah and her husband did on their deck. They put up *No Trespassing* signs all along the property line between their houses facing Sarah's yard. They spread false rumors to the other neighbors about Sarah and her husband. Sarah and her husband finally resorted to taking their neighbors to court. They won. However, that didn't stop the neighbors' offensive behavior. They did not comply with court orders. Sarah was stressed by their behavior and by all the legal things they had to do regarding their lawsuit. Of course, they had to pay a lawyer to represent them, which was costly. She dreaded all the work and court appearances involved.

Sarah's plight taught me some lessons. Never would I let people take advantage of me in the workplace like that. I would make sure my managers and coworkers understood boundaries between my willingness to go the extra mile and abuse. Sarah never felt that it was her place to object to the unreasonable demands of people in positions of authority. She worked hard to prove she was worth the long overdue promotion that the Deputy Office Director had finally pushed through for her. But she didn't believe in herself. So much was accomplished in that office because of her. If only she acknowledged her greatness and loved herself first. But what do you do about neighbors like she had? You could tell that they did not have character or integrity by the fact that they were cheating the federal government in their jobs. They were not willing to sit down and have a meeting of the minds with their neighbors. What they did to Sarah and her husband was continual and intentional harassment. And to what end? Sarah and her husband could not escape the harassment unless they were willing to move. The lesson here—check out your potential neighbors before buying a house? But Sarah and her husband had lived in their house a while before the harassment began. I don't have an answer to this one except to ignore the acts of harassment, which is pretty hard to do for even a saintly person. This is where trust in an entity greater than ourselves comes in—God, the Universe, whatever your inclinations are toward. Trust that we are being taught a lesson in life that we need to learn. Trust that we will be taken care of as meant to be.

Different people react differently to environments that others may thrive in. More and more persons are experiencing environmental stress and are developing illness, mental or physical. My friend Sarah kept pushing herself to please people in authority. She reacted to her neighbors' cold-hearted harassment with stress and more work to protect herself. Because of the stress she was under, she developed heart disease, which took her life.

When I saw my friend Sarah's face the week before she died, I knew something was very wrong. Maybe having lunch with me that day would have given her the break she needed to rejuvenate and return to work less stressed. Maybe venting with me would have relieved some of the tenseness she held inside. I will never know if my analysis is correct; I have to accept that it was her time to go. But I will surely use her early death as an example of what *not* to do if you want to keep enjoying living and loving.

Another example of a good person who put up with abuse in the work place is Fran. She and I were program managers working for the same company in the federal government "office from hell." Fran had been working in the office for a couple years when I was hired. The government Office Director had specifically requested her to be the Program Manager. Within the three short months that I worked there, I found out why. Fran took a lot of abuse from the government personnel. She was always on call, she had no backup, she supervised a large number of technical people— too large, and she was always first in line for blame when something went wrong with the office's IT support. Sometimes the government managers were downright rude and condescending to her. Her secret was to work day and night and never to take a day off. When I came in as the second Program Manager, she warned me about the Office Director and tried to coach me on how to survive in the toxic environment. The secret was to keep your mouth shut and do as you are told. Well, from the beginning, I knew that was not my style. But I tried my best. When the Office Director chastised us at meetings, I kept my mouth shut and let Fran do the talking, since she was the favored one. It still didn't work, though. The Office Director could see right through me and intuitively knew that I wasn't on board with his tyrannical management style. I lasted three months there while Fran remained. I thought highly of Fran. She is a good person and tries to please everyone. I even think it took courage to work in that toxic environment. But I refused to do what Fran did. Because of that, I could not work in that office. I stood out. After three months, I was terminated at the request of the Office Director. He told my bosses that he wanted a software engineer instead of another Program Manager. Poor Fran was back to doing everything herself again.

Aggression/Bullying

An overdose of male, aggressive energy is macho, controlling, unbalanced, and unnatural. The problem is that aggressive energy is what we've all been taught to respect…We've created a fight mentality. We're always fighting for something…

—Marianne Williamson, *A Return to Love*

These are powerful words to think about. I see two applications of these words to current events. First, look at the popularity of Donald Trump. There is no doubt that Donald Trump exudes aggressive energy. He is macho and controlling. That is what his followers admire about him. He is going to protect them and make things happen. Our fear-ridden society is reaching out to someone who they think will protect them from our enemies—terrorists, illegal immigrants who use up our resources, big government, lying Democrats, and so on. But reasoning would make us question whether Donald Trump, displaying an overinflated ego, can really or is really interested in taking care of other people besides himself. Untempered male, aggressive energy is hard. It needs to be tempered by female energy. Donald Trump's wife, Melania, found it necessary to tell the 2016 Republican National Convention that her husband has a soft side, too. Trump's words and public speeches incite us to fight our enemies and win! Winning by annihilating them? That is what they are trying to do to us! And we are condemning them for it. So are our emotions of fear getting away from us? Are we giving up emotional intelligence in desperation to appease our fears and trust a macho leader who will fight for us and make us secure? One of the quotes made by Governor Giuliani broadcast on public radio was: "Our enemy is radical Islamic terrorists…Would you trust Hillary Clinton to protect you?" Thinking that our president will or will not protect us is a stretch of the presidency's power and ability. I liken Donald Trump to so many managers I had as a federal employee that were self-absorbed and self-promoting, so much so that they did not know how to lead, support, and motivate the federal workforce to accomplish government missions to serve the public. I still see the value of a humble leader as described in the book *Good to Great*.

My supervisor when I was a research meteorologist in Missouri for the federal government was a sensitive, caring person. He was Japanese Hawaiian and had experienced discrimination in his lifetime, especially right after World War II. He was a humble man and tried to support his subordinates in his office the best he could. He was dedicated to the mission of the office. He was intelligent and a good leader. He authored or co-authored many scientific papers, taught methodology to scientists all over the world, taught college courses in meteorology, and even mentored me as a college student. He touched a lot of lives and had a positive influence on them. He made a large contribution to the organization and to humanity. I remember that he had hard times when his supervisor embarked on his own personal agenda and did things that hurt our organization. My boss got the shingles; he was so stressed by his boss's behavior and held it all inside. My boss exhibited emotional intelligence both as a person and as a manager.

The other interesting thing about Marianne Williamson's quote above is that we are always fighting for something. It is understood. I think that is true about all mankind. When I was growing up, we were fighting communism. Then we were fighting El Qaeda and radical Islam. Now we are fighting hatred and discrimination. When I was growing up, we were fighting for women's rights. We are still fighting for them today. When I was growing up, we were fighting for civil rights. We are still fighting for them today. The problem, again, here is that people sometimes abandon emotional intelligence and justify how they fight for a cause. On July 8, 2016, five policemen were gunned down by Micah Johnson, an army reservist who had served time in Afghanistan. Just about ten days later, ex-Marine Gavin Long shot and killed three policemen in Baton Rouge. The day after the Dallas shooting, Long posted a video on social media saying: "There is a time for peace and a time for war. There are times if you want peace you have to go to war." I'm sure he was taught that in the military. It appears that Long just turned his war on terrorists to war on white cops. His cause, of course, was stopping the killing of black Americans by American policemen. The fact that he believes that killing cops is going to further his cause is just not emotionally intelligent. In *Everyday Grace*, Marianne Williamson said, "...the anger that feeds our political passions can be the very thing that invalidates us in the eyes of those we must wish to persuade."

People in the military are trained to be soldiers, fighters, and killers. Most enter the military at a young, vulnerable age when they are easily taught and can adopt a new philosophy of life. But what happens when these soldiers leave the military and no longer are doing what they were trained to do—fight and kill? For many, it is not an easy transition. They have to be reincorporated into society where aggression and constant wariness is not a way of life. Have you noticed the number of lone wolf mass shooters that were trained in our own military? You all have heard the expression, "Once a Marine, always a Marine"? If a Marine becomes a manager in private industry, does s/he abandon the principles s/he was taught in the military? I worked with a lot of ex-Air Force officers in the federal government. Many still acted as if they were in the military—strict about rank among the troops, yelling commands at subordinates, publicly shaming subordinates that fail to carry out orders as expected, and so on. At one time, an ex-general in the air force was hired as the head of a federal organization I worked for. He thought he was still a general and continued to use military tactics to run the organization. He had so many Equal Employment Opportunity (EEO) complaints (which is how federal employees deal with emotionally immature people) against him, he was reprimanded by his superiors and told to stand down. I believe that morale among the employees in that organization reached an all-time low during that time. I watched as people with hunched shoulders and heads down walked into the building. I believe that veterans departing military service would benefit from a course in emotional intelligence as a first step in their transition to civilian life.

Marianne's quote applies to both men and women. I've known women managers who exhibited this aggressive energy. It is what got them into higher-paying jobs. And getting into higher-paying jobs is a sign of success in our society. Of course, people had names for these type of women, while they did not for similar men.

I once had a boss who was a bully and had other issues. As a federal employee, I was the Chief of Staff to the CIO of a federal organization. The CIO came from private industry, and, as I learned, he became a federal CIO to "beef up" his resume. At first, he was full of ideas and was eager to improve IT in the organization. From the start, though, he was stern and unforgiving. When I first started working for him, I was immediately stressed, so much so that I got the shingles. Each time I went into his office for a meeting with him, the nerves in my back wrenched. One day it was so bad, the CIO's secretary took me to the building nurse. When they could not explain what was happening, I went to a walk-in doctor's office. The doctor told me that I had the shingles. I never took a day off. The pain and exhaustion were draining, but I never let on that I wasn't feeling well. I refused to let him know he got to me.

After a year, the CIO changed his agenda to serving only himself and doing only things that made a name for himself. He made and implemented decisions that only served himself and disrespected his top managers. One of his tactics was to send several people to execute the same task without telling any of them that there were others doing the same thing. Of course, they eventually stumbled upon each other and were confused as to what was going on and what they should do. The CIO changed the rules on a daily basis so that he was the only one who knew what was going on and was in control. One day, he told me that he was going to do something that affected his top managers. I told him that his managers would not like it. He responded by saying loudly in a forceful voice, "I don't care what they think. It's all about me! Me, me, me!" I thought, *At least he was honest.* But how immature was that? One time I presented him with a report he had requested and he was not happy with the content that his top managers had prepared. He rejected it and threw it at me. The next morning, when we had our regular meeting, he said, "I crossed the line yesterday, didn't I." I said, "Yes, you did." Soon after that, he realized that I was onto his selfish, bullying behavior. So what did he do? He got rid of me. He sent me on a detail to one of his executives. She didn't know what to do with me exactly. She had a contractor who did her bidding. So I had nothing to do except things that the CIO still needed from me. Eventually, I asked him if I could work for him exclusively again. He said he would take me back "only if you don't think." What? Again, his honesty bowled me over. That didn't last long, and he found another of his executives who was "most cooperative" with him to detail me to. And what did this manager tell me to do? She told me that she had no idea what her people did, so she wanted me to find out. I had to interview her disgruntled employees to find out what they did. Of course, I had to tell them what I was doing and why, so they were even more disgruntled with their manager. I was eventually able to escape that office by applying to the agency Senior Executive Service Candidate Development Program. The program developed people for the next step in rank above the GS-15. For the program, I was able to choose and work on a detail outside the organization. That was a fun year. I must add, though, that the CIO tried to prevent the program from accepting me. The program leaders, however, did not accept his objections to my application. Individuals were allowed to apply to the program without their supervisors' knowledge or consent.

At one point, working for the CIO, I was so desperate I did a search on the Internet using some of his behavior. To my surprise, there was an entire website dedicated to bully bosses. It described their behavior as psychotic and controlling. It was a perfect match to my boss's behavior. This was the first time that I accepted that bosses could have mental and emotional disorders that explained their emotionally immature behavior. The only solution the website offered was to change jobs and escape the bad behavior. Some of the current websites that provide insight to bully bosses and advice on how to deal with them are:

- "When the Boss is a Bully" by *Psychology Today*: https://www. psychologytoday.com/articles/199509/when-the-boss-is-bully
- "8 Signs Your Boss is a Bully" by Verywell: https://www.verywell. com/signs-your-boss-is-a-bully-460785
- "How to Deal with a Bully Boss" by *Forbes*: http://www.forbes.com/sites/ lizryan/2015/02/20/how-to-deal-with-a-bully-boss/#2d8b4ca02942

CIO.com offers this information:

> "It is hard to predict when you are being hired by a bully
> boss because they usually can turn on the charm when

needed as in an interview. So you won't know until it is too late. The most popular solution is to start looking for another job immediately when you got him/her figured out as a bully. Is your boss a tyrant of Machiavellian proportions? If it makes you feel better, you're not alone. According to a study by the Employment Law Alliance, almost half of all employees have been targeted by a bully boss."

The study also revealed the following:

- Eighty-one percent of bullies are managers.
- Fifty percent of bullies are women, and 50 percent are men.
- Eighty-four percent of targets are women.
- Eighty-two percent of targets ultimately lost their job.
- Ninety-five percent of bullying is witnessed.

It is interesting that 95 percent of bullying is witnessed. You would think that the bully's superiors would hold the bully responsible for his/her emotionally immature behavior. From this, it appears that bullying in the workplace is not condemned as it should be in many places.

If you read and use the principles of Asian philosophies, you will bend and not resist when someone pushes you. Have you ever seen two dogs confront each other? The alpha will make a threatening gesture, and the other dog will roll on his/her back and expose his/her underside saying that he/she doesn't want to fight and gives in. I've noticed this behavior in my two male cats. When one is the aggressor, the other runs to get away. If he is cornered under a chair, he hisses and tries to defend himself. He flees to get away at the first opportunity or stays his ground until the aggressor tires of threatening him. If a human uses a similar technique, it requires giving up the ego and exposing one's vulnerability. First step should be to flee from the aggressor. If you are cornered or trapped, defend yourself the best you can but flee at the first possible opportunity.

In the case of road rage, the obvious thing to do is to get out of the aggressor's way. If you see someone behind or next to you exhibiting aggressive driving behavior, get out of the way! Do not continue as if s/he isn't there. A couple times, I've actually witnessed women poking along in the passing lane on the Beltway with a man in a big truck riding her bumper. She continues onward as if no one was there. That's just ludicrous! I want to yell at her, "Get out of his way! He won't quit until he teaches you a lesson!" Remember your defensive driving in driver's education? You should always be aware of the drivers surrounding you and predict what they might do next. Aggressive drivers are dangerous, so stay away from them. If s/he is bent on teaching you a lesson, pull to the side and stop. If s/he still pursues you, roll up the windows, lock the doors, and call 911. The important thing to remember is that you do not know what the aggressor is capable of. And maybe s/he doesn't know either. One thing is sure, though: you don't want to find out.

If the aggressor is a bully on social media, this is a tough situation. Many people believe everything they see on the Internet. So mean-spirited people can tarnish your reputation. There are even companies now that serve to protect your reputation on the Internet. It takes a lot of self-assurance to ignore attacks on social media. Most of us don't have the amount of self-assurance it takes to ignore attacks and fluff them off. Most of us would react and panic that they are ruining our reputation. But still the best reaction is no reaction. Do not give credence to the attacks. You will just have to make sure that enough people surrounding you know your virtues so that, eventually, they will know that the attacker is the one with the problem, not you. I learned a good tactic from Selena Gomez on the *Ellen DeGeneres Show*. A picture of her in a bathing suit on the beach went virile. Of course, there are always the critics who commented that she looked fat. When Ellen asked her how she responded, she said, "I responded by saying that I am happy with myself." How cool! Of course, it takes a sense of maturity and emotional intelligence to say something like that and mean it. If you do not resist, it takes the fun out of bullying for the bully. Most young people do not have and have not yet acquired the self-assuredness that this response requires. That is why learning and practicing emotional intelligence is so important. In a lot of cases, it is advantageous not to take ourselves and our critics too seriously.

Bullying is singling out another person as different and trying to discredit him/her using social media, gossip, and exclusion. I heard on public radio a mother's account of how she perceived her daughter as a potential bully and redirected her to avoid hurtful bullying activity. She described what tipped her off. She said her daughter told her a girl at school was following her around and pestering her. The mother said, "You mean she has been trying to be your friend?" The daughter responded saying that the girl was "annoying" her. The mother picked up on the way she said the word *annoying*. She knew her daughter was popular in school and intuitively knew that this could turn into a situation where her daughter and her friends single out the annoying girl and bully her. So the mother challenged her daughter to talk to the girl and report back five things that she liked about her. The daughter responded, "No way." So the mother refused to take the daughter to school until she agreed to the challenge. The mother did not take her daughter to school until 2:00 p.m. the next day when the daughter finally agreed to do as the mother asked. That just meant that the daughter had less time to talk to the girl and learn five things about her. The mother said that she thought that her daughter talked to the girl in the carpool line after school, but she did report five things she liked about her. And they ended up being best friends through school. The mother said that she was challenged by other mothers saying that they didn't dictate who their children should be friends with and how. But this mother responded by saying, "You tell your children that they have to brush their teeth and eat greens. Why can't you guide them in the area of social interactions?" How would it be if all mothers were this attentive and wise to give their children guidance like this? I dare to say that with our hands-off methods of letting children make their own choices and learn in the school of hard knocks, this type of parenting is in the minority. How many parents are shocked when they learn that their child is a bully or a victim of bullying? Not to say the parents are in the wrong, but to say that with so many tools for impersonal communication and information sharing at their fingertips, it is harder and more important to monitor children's activities more closely. Tools such as cell phones and social media are not always used in a thoughtful manner by many adults, let alone by children who have not fully developed emotionally and socially. (Another selling point for teaching emotional intelligence in schools).

Having worked in a science-oriented federal organization, I was bullied more times than I could ever list by male managers and my male counterparts. I was even bullied by some of the few women that made it to high positions in the organization. (That's why these women got to high positions—they even scared the men). But I never let it stop or discourage me. Once or twice, I hurried out of the room to safety when I stood up to a man who was bullying me! I always did the best work I could. And no matter what my enemies said about me, they could not deny that I was the hardest-working person they knew. Of course, they called me names like "workaholic" and told people I just loved working hard, like it was an insult. But, again, I was true to my number-one values—honesty and responsibility. So my best advice to those who are bullied is to keep doing what you are doing that can be labeled objectively as the right thing to do. You may not be popular, but the truth about you will be known in the end.

One tactic I employed immediately when I realized someone was directing bad behavior toward me, or one of my employees was exhibiting bad behavior, was to document it. I kept a log of the dates and times and descriptions of the bad behavior. I saved e-mails from them that were proof of the bad behavior. You never know when you will need to show authorities proof of the bad behavior. Most of the time, I didn't need to use my documentation, but there were times I did. In addition, most of the time I made sure at least one other person, whom I could trust and confide in, knew what was going on. I never knew when I would need a witness and character reference.

One time, as a federal employee, I was being harassed by the new CIO in a large federal agency and his Deputy. Since I had been the previous CIO's right-hand person, the new administration and their appointees did not trust me. They had different designs for me and my work than my previous supervisor had. In fact, the Deputy wanted my job. They resorted to bullying me, I guess, so I would leave. I began forwarding their e-mails to the manager of the EEO office. She advised me that the only recourse I had was to file an EEO complaint against them and to say that they were discriminating against me because I was a woman (even though one of the aggressors was a woman). I did what she said. She was then able to get me a facilitated mediation session. This was very productive. I was able to tell the CIO what I wanted—a position with a title and recognition of my authority in that position. He complied. He provided me a new job and title, and the harassment stopped. I set upon my new job and was relieved when the harassment stopped. It wasn't long after that, though, that I was able to escape the environment and started working at another federal organization.

One word of advice I would give to young people experiencing bullying in the workplace: make sure people know how hard you are working and how good you are at your job. If you can, take on visible projects where everyone can't help but see how well you are doing. Be on the lookout for small projects that no one else wants that can bring you easy wins and visibility. People in administrative jobs can do things like issue office newsletters and write articles about office successes that they orchestrated. They can send out office e-mails that communicate vital information for the troops and that convey that they are on top of things. These types of actions protect you from any one bully discrediting you. Other people won't see any negative things the bully says about you.

Negativity/Exclusion

Some individuals see other people's differences as a negative rather than a positive. I loved my mother, but I was always amazed at how she could not understand when people did not think like she did. She would say, "How can people think like that?" I would say, "Because they are not you!" She would just shake her head. She was shocked when I, her daughter, expressed thoughts that were different from her beliefs. She thought that, since I was her daughter, I was supposed to be like her and think like her. I do give her credit, though. As both of us grew, she learned more and more to accept my differences and others' differences. She was my role model of compassion for others. Her friends needed her more than she needed them.

If people regard differences as negatives, they most often try to rid themselves of those negatives and the people who stand for them. This leads to exclusion. How many people do you know that say, "That person is different than me. I need to get to know him/her better to understand them?" Sounds ludicrous, doesn't it? But emotional intelligence says you need to be open to others to understand them and have compassion for them. At least, if you are not going to make the effort to know and understand them, do not judge them. You cannot know what they are thinking or what they have been through.

For the biggest part of my career, I worked in a culture that a person just had to say something bad (usually untrue) about someone else, and people believed it and acted on it. False rumors could spread so quickly. People did not bother to check out the facts. Maybe years later the truth became known, but by then it was too late. The subject person was already defamed and ruined. A person's reputation could so easily be smeared. If the person countered the attack, then people just said they were being defensive and thought even less of the person. I found this behavior frustrating. I was incredulous that managers did not make the effort to check out their source of misinformation before using it as a basis for decisions. A person might not be hired for a job because someone with a personal agenda (against them) said something that incriminated the person. And there was *always* someone out to get you in government. I suppose it took too much time and effort to investigate the facts. To me, this is emotional immaturity. It is acting on emotions—fear—rather than facts or reasoning.

When I was in grade school, I was never invited to the parties the girls in my class held and attended. It profoundly affected me then and influenced my behavior in high school. I still think of it today. But I didn't realize why until recently I was watching the *Today Show*. The *Today Show* had a guest who was overweight growing up. She was asked if it was an issue when she was young. She said yes, that the other girls never included her in their parties and activities. A lightbulb went on. I thought, *That could be one of the reasons why I was never included in the girls' parties and activities in grade school! I was overweight!* Another reason could be that I was a "nerd." That is something I've come to understand and accept about myself. I'm fine with it. That, however, distinguished me from the "socialites." Funny enough, although I was aware that this was happening, it was never a source of angst or depression for me. I never once gave it a thought that it was because I was overweight or a nerd, even though that might have been the reason. Why? Because I associated with other girls who were nerds and slightly overweight, and we had a good time ourselves. I had crushes on many of the boys and had fun with them instead. The girls I associated with seemed like real people to me—girls who looked deeper than appearances when choosing friends. The boys I associated with didn't care that I was a nerd and were not concerned with appearances. I cannot recall what I used to talk about with grade-school boys, but I do remember that another boy and I were the only ones who admitted we were talking when the teacher left the room and asked who had talked when she returned. When I think about it, I seemed like a doofus, essentially opening myself up to punishment when most of the other talkers did not. But honesty and responsibility were big for me and always have been. And back then, integrity was recognized. I was the recipient of the American Legion award to the eighth-grade girl who exhibited the most character and leadership potential.

Years later when I attended a ten-year grade-school reunion, I found out that the same girls who snubbed me in grade school snubbed me as a grown woman. But the difference was that I understood and did not care. I was married, slim, and self-confident then. I understood that these women excluded other people who did not appear to be like themselves. They would always be that way. My life, however, opened up in high school. I slimmed down and became more outgoing. In high school, I was surrounded by many girls who were like me—inclusive and fun loving. I will never know the real reason the girls in grade school in my class were so exclusive. But I understand and accept that there are people like that. I just don't need to associate with them, and I don't need to feel bad about it. On the up side, the same boys that talked with me in grade school were welcoming at the reunion.

In the previous section, I mentioned that I joined the Senior Executive Service Candidate Development Program. The sad fact is that, although federal agencies execute these programs and create a pool of trained, qualified Senior Executive Service (SES) candidates, these candidates are seldom selected to fill vacant SES positions in the agency. Instead, agency executives more often select applicants from outside their own agency who are more like them. In other words, qualified, trained persons working in their own agency are excluded from the SES while persons who have not been trained are selected. Granted that the selected candidate may be trained in some other training program once s/he is on board, but that is not the norm. This practice creates an exclusive group of executives at the top in federal agencies without diversity. Those in control maintain control by not allowing differences of opinion and different ways of doing things. And, the outside candidate selected has not been trained in the principles of the agency for excellent managers (and neither have the selecting officials). The Development Program, then, is ineffective; it is just a means to check a box and make the Human Resources Department look good. In my career as a federal employee, I saw one exception to the practice of not assigning Development Program graduates SES positions. One year, the Development Program ended just prior to the start of a new administration headed by the "other party." To spite the other party and introduce diversity into the SES ranks, the Deputy Secretary of the agency in which I worked at the time assigned every one of the Program graduates to an SES position in the agency. Many of the graduates were women and people of color. That was the only time I saw all of the Development Program graduates actually work in SES positions. Having retired from federal government service and having worked for many different companies since, I see that this is also how company executives maintain control and push their own agenda—by only hiring people like themselves and excluding people that would introduce diversity. While I understand that private companies have the right to push and maintain the company agenda, I would think that the federal government's mission is to best serve all of the American people, not just a certain group. The American people, in my mind, would best be served if the managers of federal agencies reflected the same diversity that is found in the population of the country.

Narcissism

In his book *Sane Society*, Erich Fromm says of narcissism:

> "For the narcissistically involved person, there is only one reality, that of his own thought processes, feelings and needs. The world outside is not experienced or perceived objectively, i.e., as existing in its own terms, conditions, and needs."

Fromm relates extreme narcissism to insanity and love to sanity and freedom. Narcissists allow their egos to control their interactions with others.

In our growing population, more and more people are becoming narcissistic to protect themselves and ensure that they get what they need. Some people become predators, using others as a means to accomplish their own agendas. They lack empathy for others and have no qualms about taking from others all they can get. Scammers are a good example. They prey on the elderly who are trusting and don't know better, and it doesn't even phase them. We just need to be wary at all times that predators are everywhere. We need to make sure that we don't fall victim to them.

In the case that a person is narcissistic, s/he will emote or react in a manner that serves only the self. In that situation, others likely will get hurt. Therefore, we need to think before we react. We need to try to anticipate whether the receiver of our reaction will be hurt by it in any way. If we predict that the receiver, in any way, might be hurt by our reaction, we must delay our reaction as long as we need to, to think through a reaction that will not hurt the receiver. When I first became a manager, several people accused me of having emotions that I did not feel when I sent them an e-mail. I reread my e-mails to them and realized how they could misinterpret my words to mean something other than what I had meant. From then on, I reread my e-mails before sending them to make sure my tone and intent could not easily be misinterpreted.

There is a woman in the neighborhood with whom I had a seven-year friendship. In fact, she lived in the basement of my house when she rented out her house for short-term vacation rentals. I recognized that she needed this in order to make a living and did not charge her for either rent or utility expenses. She responded by buying me little things and doing things for me like sitting with my cats when I went on vacation. But after she had a garage built with a second level to stay in and no longer needed the use of my basement while she rented her house, she became self-absorbed and too busy to make time for me. I'm not sure if that was a conscious effort to distance herself or if she wanted to assert her independence since she no longer needed me. With the break in association, I stepped back and looked objectively at our relationship. I was able to identify negatives that had been showing up for me all along. I saw that she spent a lot of time in self-promotion. If I disagreed with anything she said, I would never say so because she was the self-declared expert in everything and was always right. She was vocal about expressing her opinions; to her, her views were the right views. It would only cause conflict if I expressed a different view. She often withheld information from me about what she was doing. I didn't give it a second thought. I figured if she wanted me to know, she would tell me. I didn't want to pry. She had some paranoia and obsessions that she exhibited, but I never responded when she would talk about them. I did not want to be judgmental. In other words, I was not being true to myself in my relationship with her. I was suppressing my thoughts and feelings for the sake of peace. When the friendship ended suddenly, I blamed her for hurting me. Throughout the relationship, she said and did things that were hurtful. At first they appeared to be benign because she was just being herself, but during the last year or so, they seemed more deliberate. I eventually realized, though, that I was the one who chose to end the relationship. To me, her narcissistic behavior indicated that she did not value our friendship or who I was. Whenever I confided my feelings with her, she could not empathize with me. We communicated by e-mail only in the end, and I just stopped responding when her e-mails exhibited more lack of empathy and self-promotion. Though I felt the hurt for a long while, I reasoned that her behavior prevented us, in my mind, from sharing honest and open communication. Her reality was different from mine. So, really, the breakup was a matter of time. I can accept that it is her choice to put herself first. I figured she deserved that. Or maybe she was unconsciously using survival techniques learned when she was young. Whatever her motivation, I can accept it. I suspect that she had some internal issues or fears that she had not worked out. But I just could not accept a relationship where both of us were not our true selves. I let it go and am grateful for the things both of us learned and gained while friends.

Another thing I have noticed about narcissistic people is that they have a constant need for admiration. If someone doesn't give it to them, they either try to degrade the other person in some way or write him/her off. Narcissists have to be number one. In a group, they make sure they stand out in some way. They have to be in charge or they don't want to play. They don't join groups; they only lead them. With these characteristics, you can see why some narcissistic people rise to be managers. They don't want to take orders; they want to give them. They feel they are entitled to be in charge. Narcissistic managers push their own agendas, and their subordinates become aggravated and disillusioned when their needs and the needs of the office mission are overlooked. Rules that apply to others don't apply to them.

My friend Kurt and his brother were narcissistic. I was often shocked at Kurt's brother's brutal honesty with the women in his life. I saw him say hurtful things if something they gave him or did for him wasn't what he wanted or expected. I thought, *Couldn't he have just said thank you and not pointed out the gift's deficiency?* As with the case above, Kurt's narcissism gave me a feeling that our friendship wasn't valued, that I wasn't valued as a person. I was constantly suppressing who I was to keep peace and let him be in charge. When I no longer provided Kurt with the admiration he needed, he moved on. While Kurt and I were together, I checked out the National Institute of Mental Health's website. At the time, they had a helpful description of narcissistic behavior. They have changed their website, and the description of that disorder and others is no longer there. But the website, at that time, helped me understand what I was dealing with. At the same time, I read Daniel Goleman's *Destructive Emotions*.

His book confirmed for me what I was dealing with and helped me to understand that Kurt's emotions were destructive for both him and me. What I learned from Daniel Goleman's book and my experience with Kurt helped prepare me and helped me understand what was going on with my relationship with my neighbor friend. Although I learned a lot during my relationships with Kurt and my neighbor, I couldn't say that that their friendships provided what my soul needed. It was fun while it lasted. Well, they had their moments.

I was an only child. When I was growing up, it was not uncommon when people asked you if you had brothers and sisters, if you responded, "I am an only child," they would say, "Spoiled, huh?" Of course, this was an unfair generalization. But I think my mother must have been determined not to raise a spoiled child (whatever that entailed). From her German heritage, she learned the value of discipline. She beat into my head (that's figurative, of course) that I should never be selfish, that I should always be aware of when I could help and care for other people. She set a stellar example of that.

Managing Self

To begin with, it is important to realize and remember that we get back what we put out there. This is reason enough for us to ensure that we rid ourselves of destructive emotions. This does not mean that we have to be happy all the time. There are times when we are hurt, sad, or are grieving, but those emotions are not destructive. We have to work through those emotions in time. I'm talking about if we put hatred out there, we will get hatred back. If we put love out there, we will get love in return. I can still remember days going to work and I felt so good about myself and about my life. I emanated happiness. People I didn't even know would talk to me as I passed them on the street. The question is, how do we manage our emotions so that we emanate and surround ourselves with love and happiness?

In *Everyday Grace*, Marianne Williamson said: "People telepathically register your real thoughts, regardless of whether you are consciously aware of them or not." How well I know this. To top it off, my facial expressions clearly indicate what is going on in my head and heart. I just can't hide my emotions. I think that is why people with different values than I have avoided me, while people with the same values are attracted to me. I think people know right away if I don't respect them and they immediately go on the attack. They think that they best be on the offensive in case I make the first move. But they are only projecting their own fears. Since they avoid me, they don't get to know me, and they assume that I will behave as they would.

We all just want to be happy. There are many books written on how to achieve happiness. The Dalai Lama wrote at least two books on happiness: *The Dalai Lama's Big Book of Happiness* and *The Art of Happiness: A Handbook for Living*. But as Marianne Williamson said, "Happiness is an acquired skill" (*Everyday Grace*). She said there is always something to complain about in the best of times and something to celebrate in the worst of times. So maintaining a state of happiness is something we learn how to do by working on our state of mind. It takes many years of practice.

My mother lived to be a hundred years old. People are curious and ask me what her secret to longevity was. I attribute it to her attitude. She was a caring, positive person. She loved life and just being. She enjoyed people but also was complete in herself and liked being alone. She acknowledged the darkness of the world but refused to let it bring her down. She made her living space something she enjoyed and was proud of. She was realistic about who she was and when it was time to go. She was a good role model for me and for her younger friends. Everyone with whom she came in contact loved her. There were many people at her hundredth birthday party.

To feel happiness, we often experience times of unhappiness. To feel compassion for others, we experience times of suffering ourselves. After we recover from a loss, we need to take inventory of the people and things we have in our lives that bring us happiness. Most of all, we need to remember how good we feel when we reach out and help another. Material things are here for our temporary amusement, but our interactions with others build our character that lasts a lifetime. A key to happiness is gratitude for the present moment—who in our life adds value and brings us happiness. In an instant, things can change; we can suffer another loss. So lest we suffer regrets, we need to appreciate the moment and those surrounding us. My mother used to say in moments of rough times, "My mother warned me that there'd be days like this," meaning life is a series of rough times, ups and downs. They pass, and we appreciate the good times. Harold Kushner said in his forward to Viktor Frankl's book, *Man's Search for Meaning*: "You cannot control what happens to you in life, but you can always control what you will feel and do about what happens to you."

This section talks about the techniques of managing ourselves that we need to practice if we have emotional intelligence. These techniques are not all inclusive, but they are some of the important ones.

Reasoning

One book that blew me away when I read it was *Sane Society* by Eric Fromm. This book brought about a turning point in my outlook on my life. It is not an easy read but well worth the effort. In *Sane Society*, Erich Fromm said:

> "In observing the quality of thinking in alienated man, it is striking to see how his intelligence has developed and how his reason has deteriorated. He takes his reality for granted…He does not even ask what is behind it, why things are the way they are, and where they are going. By intelligence I mean the ability to manipulate concepts for the purpose of achieving some practical end…Reason, on the other hand, aims at understanding: it tries to find out what is behind the surface, to recognize the kernel, the essence of reality which surrounds us…Reason is required in order to predict…and prediction sometimes is necessary even for physical survival."

I never thought about differentiating between intelligence and reasoning in that manner. In this context, I have known many people who were intelligent but did not reason. That is, they were very skilled at manipulating the situation or people to achieve their own personal agendas, but they failed to use reason to present and understand the facts of the situation or the people involved. Donald Trump is a good example of an intelligent person. He knows how to say things to get people's attention, and he knows what to say that people want to hear. But what he says so often lacks consideration of the effect it will have on other people. People with reason are able to work toward an organization's mission and goals without inserting their own agendas. Trump is not a good example of a person who uses reasoning over intelligence.

In *Sane Society*, Erich Fromm also said of reason: "The further his (man) reason develops, the more adequate becomes his system of orientation, that is, the more it approximates reality."

Emotional intelligence deals with the acknowledgment and acceptance of reality. Reason (in addition to awareness and acceptance of our feelings) gets us to the reality we need for emotional intelligence. Without reason, the ego is allowed to create whatever reality it so desires. Fromm said, "Reason is a faculty which must be practiced, in order to develop…" We must continually practice conquering the ego and the reality it creates. If we conquer the ego, we are able to control destructive emotions and use reason to relate to others. Relating to others with love, compassion, and empathy makes us and others happy.

When you were a child, did your mother ever tell you to do something, and you asked why? She responded, "Because I said so." The reason she said that was to avoid explaining to you the entire story or reasoning behind the order. It was easier and quicker to respond with fewer words. Since she was in a position of authority, you obeyed. As you matured, you were able to understand her reasoning when she issued that order. Nonetheless, it was good to practice to ask why in case your mother was open to explaining the reasoning at that time.

When I worked in the radar program in a federal organization, my boss went to visit the Eastern Region Director. To impress her and to appease her (since she was vocal and demanding and hard to get along with), he promised her immediate delivery of a Principle User Platform (PUP), which was a couple monitors and keyboard for using the radar and radar images. This achieved his purpose of making himself look good and powerful in the program and smoothing relations with the Eastern Region. However, since the Eastern Region was not scheduled to receive a PUP for months, this began a huge fiasco in the program that cost the program thousands of dollars. We called it the "PUP shuffle." Many hours were spent by many people, both federal employees and the prime contractor, revising the PUP delivery schedule. The schedule was complicated by the fact that there were different kinds of PUPs that were slated for different offices at different times. So although my boss was intelligent and manipulated the situation to his advantage, his lack of reasoning proved detrimental to the overall program.

Two other authors who talk about reasoning versus fear in terms of politics are President Jimmy Carter in *Our Endangered Values* and Vice President Al Gore in *Assault on Reason*. Both explain how politics in the States has turned to tactics using fear to govern and gain political influence. In the name of "protecting the public," politicians have been feeding the public lies and twisted truths in order to further their own personal agendas. These books are enlightening. They present the potential that using fear in politics has to misguide and influence people. Both authors stress how important it is for U.S. citizens to use reason and not take for granted what politicians with personal agendas are telling us. We need to check the facts. The facts provide us with the best approach.

The ability to reason is related to having common sense. We often speak of people who do or do not have common sense. It implies the ability to apply one's knowledge and life's past experiences in a reasonable way to current decisions or actions.

Integrity/Principles

In *Sane Society*, Erich Fromm said:

> "Ethics, at least in the meaning of Greco-Judeo-Christian tradition, is inseparable from reason. Ethical behavior is based on the faculty of making value judgments on the basis of reason; it means deciding between good and evil, and to act upon the decision...Furthermore...the aim of life is to unfold man's love and reason and that every other human activity has to be subordinated to this aim."

Learning and practicing ethics is closely related to learning and practicing emotional intelligence.

Part of emotional intelligence is having principles by which to live and having the courage to stand up for those principles. You can be sure that you will always be tested, and you will have to decide where you draw the line and refuse to compromise your principles. Lying is a means to get us in trouble. As the saying goes, *what a tangled web we weave* when we lie. People eventually learn the truth, and our reputation is tarnished. We lose trust and alienate ourselves. The alienation can lead to depression. If you are always honest, you have firm ground to stand on. No one can doubt you and your intentions. My grandmother always said, "Right is might." In other words, you are mighty if you are truthful. Which brings me to another subject ...

People get hung up on the word "right," as in they have to be right, or they are right and others are wrong. There are even jokes about being right. A good one a (male) friend at work told me is: "If a man (husband) is alone in the woods, is he still wrong?" Or men say: "Women are always right" (implying that that is what women think). As a manager, I learned that there is no right or wrong, only choices. So there is no need to get competitive about it. There are just different ways of doing things. It's more like there are "fifty shades of gray" and no black and white. Sure there are ethics and morals that dictate what is right and what is wrong in our society and what is the right thing to do as a human being connected to all other humans and the earth. But when we are talking about managing work in the office, you have choices. If you make a bad choice, you can always change course and fix any ill results that occurred with the first choice. There is always a fix for everything. It may not be easy, but there are things that can be done. As my friend John always said, "Everything always works out one way or the other."

I have noticed couples doing this: One person says something and does not totally get his/her facts straight. The other person challenges it. The first person refuses to surrender. Then they're at each other. Emotional intelligence tells us when to let it go. The expression is: *Don't sweat the small stuff.*

Lying has become passé. Today, you assume that people outside your circle of trust are feeding you a line until you see proof that what they said is true. Some of the leaders of our own country, state, or county are not to be trusted. It is understood that politicians tell the public whatever they need to in order to further their agendas and explain their actions. At other times, politicians withhold information from the public because the public wouldn't understand the circumstances under which they chose to act a certain way. In addition, the media reporting what politicians say and do may be suspect. We always need to check out the facts before believing everything the media tells us.

With an increase in population in a capitalistic culture and an increase in competition, the rules change. Integrity in the workplace decreases. People beef up their resumes and stretch the truth (in the name of competition). The government now does extensive background checks on all government employees and contractors. The background checks can take months and months. How can companies staff tasks on contracts when the government takes months to give the go-ahead to the company to bring a new employee on board? Large companies also do their own background checks. People push their own agendas at all costs when they are competing and feel threatened. In one case, I was interrogated by a contractor conducting a background check on me for a job with a large company. One of my past supervisors of whom I described earlier who tried to discredit me, lied to his management about an encounter we had, and then terminated me, reported to the investigator that I was insubordinate and he had to present me with a reprimand and then fire me. The investigator told me what my ex-supervisor said and asked me about it. I described the situation to the investigator and he decided that I wasn't really fired, that he terminated me from the position to hire someone else (his cronies) in it. He told me that he often comes across situations similar to mine in which the supervisor intentionally tries to harm the reputation of someone s/he supervised at one time and prevent them from future employment elsewhere. He told me that these people are mean-spirited and ego-driven. I felt relieved and understood. The investigator had no emotional buy-in to my case and used reason to analyze the facts.

Honesty is the best policy.

In my mind, lying is never appropriate. Well, I shouldn't say never because I became quite skilled at lying to my ninety-nine-year-old mother. I found I couldn't tell her anything I was doing because she would worry and tell me not to do it. She was so afraid of losing me. If she asked me questions related to what I was doing, I would make up something that she would accept. I never liked doing this, but I justified it by telling myself I was protecting her. I was probably really just protecting myself. But other than those few situations where the truth really causes harm, honesty is one of the principles of emotional intelligence—honesty with ourselves and with others. The saying *honesty is the best policy* has not lost its pertinence.

Courage/Motivation

It takes courage to live and work in this world. It is hard to find someone who we relate to on a deeper level than just living in the same neighborhood and having kids who go to the same school. When we are married, it takes courage to live together as a couple and work through issues that arise. It takes courage to confront the other when it is appropriate and to do so in a manner that leads to resolution rather than alienation. It takes courage to live or be alone. It is preferable over the alternative of spending time with people who mistreat us or who we can't relate to. Sure we are connected via social media, but what satisfaction does that provide us when we feel down emotionally, when we feel that no one understands us?

Stand firm on your principles.

It takes courage to stand firm on your principles. I didn't think about it at the time, but there were many times that I had to have courage to take a stand for my principles in my career. I look back and think how brave I had to be, but at the time, I was just trying to survive while not compromising my principles of honesty and responsibility. It was a no-brainer for me. I encountered many examples of exclusion and disrespect.

I became a manager in a federal program for the acquisition of weather equipment. I was the Acquisition Manager, and a woman who was very difficult to get along with was the Program Manager. She was very tight with the Contracting Officer. Everyone wondered if they were sleeping together, which would not have been an ethical thing to do. One evening, I received a call from the Contracting Officer. He told me that he had a terrible headache and he didn't have any painkillers in the house. Could I bring him some? I was terribly concerned about him and rushed over there with a bottle of painkillers. While I was there, he made a pass at me and kissed me. I was shocked! I told him that I had to keep things on a business level only. (And besides, what would the Program Manager think if we had a love triangle?) The next morning at work, he would not look at me or talk to me. From then on, both he and the Program Manager did everything they could to make my life miserable. Who knows what the Contracting Officer told the Program Manager—most likely that I made a pass at him and he rejected me. I made appointments to talk to the Program Manager, and she canceled them. They both refused to communicate with me or cooperate with me. I was basically on my own, and they looked for opportunities to make me look bad. At times, I was so distressed I cried to relieve tension. I remember describing the Contracting Officer's behavior to his supervisor on the phone, all the while crying. She said nothing to comfort me and give me hope which told me that she was powerless to affect a change. At appraisal time, although I had turned the program around and saw that it ended on time and on budget, my supervisor gave me the lowest favorable rating. He apologized and said he had to give me that because it was no secret the difficulties I had getting along with the Program Manager. I was incredulous that he had no backbone and succumbed to appearances to protect himself. Not only was I mistreated by the Program Manager and Contracting Officer, I was abandoned by my own chain of command and provided no support whatsoever. I didn't need the acknowledgment from my boss, though. I knew that I had done good things for the program, things that probably would not have gotten done if I had not taken charge. (Emotional intelligence is recognizing and embracing your own good motives and accomplishments). Luckily, the program ended, and I moved on to another job—another job with the same boss in my chain of command, though.

After the program ended in which I was the Acquisition Manager, I was placed by federal managers in a group of engineers, a team of several GS-15s with which they didn't know what to do after their programs ended. The political appointee in charge of the organization assigned the Acquisitions Office Director, my previous boss, the task of putting a team together to conduct a study or investigation on where to locate a new federal building to house a large number of federal employees. Of course, the Director delegated this study to one of his engineers who happened to be my new boss. Neither my boss nor the delegated Director wanted to take on the study or deal with the hard work. So my boss delegated the study to me. I was given an initial list of people to include on the study team by the Director. The first thing I did, which made complete sense to me, was to schedule a meeting with the Office Directors of the two offices who had employees who would move into the new building. I wanted to ask them their views of where they thought their people should be located. I called them and asked them when they could meet. The first Director defaulted to his representative on the study team and said he didn't need to meet. I talked with the other Director's secretary, and she scheduled a meeting with him. Right after that, my Office Director's Deputy came running over to my office to tell me to cancel the meeting I had scheduled. I wasn't there, thankfully, but the office secretary told me what he said. Later, when I talked with him, the Deputy told me that I wasn't allowed, as a GS-15, to talk with the Office Directors I had called since they were SES employees (the next higher rank in government service). He told me to cancel the meeting that had been arranged. Here, the same people who didn't want anything to do with the work were now telling me how to do my job. I called the Director's secretary who had scheduled the meeting. She told me that the Director was looking forward to the meeting and she didn't want to cancel it. So we left the meeting on his schedule, and nothing more was said.

My Office Director's Deputy attended the meeting I led, and we all shared valuable information. The Director for whom the meeting was arranged was grateful for the opportunity to voice his opinions (and that someone was listening to them). Afterwards, my Office Director's Deputy said, "That was a good meeting!" I agreed (holding my tongue from saying what I really wanted to say). I was successful at bringing the team together and conducting the study to determine the most appropriate location for the new building. But at a meeting with my Office Director to update him on progress, he accused me of not following protocol and a host of other things that I can't remember because I stopped listening. That did it for me. I deliberately and calmly tore into him and said that I was working hard and bringing things together that neither he nor my boss wanted to do, and everyone on the team was happy with the way things were going. I told him he ought to be thanking me profusely for my hard work and dedication and leading the study for him. Suddenly, he changed his tune and started thanking me for everything I reported at the meeting. I was shocked. Afterwards, his Deputy scolded me for standing up to the Director like that. All the time I was telling the Director off, his Deputy had been sinking lower and lower in his chair. I just said that I wasn't going to let him talk to me like that when I was working so hard and so successfully. I knew my own mind and knew when it was appropriate to speak up. We left it at that. Neither one of them bothered me after that incident. I delivered the report on time, and our recommendation was implemented.

From these experiences, I found that I had nothing to fear. I stood up for myself and for my principles when I was able. But not all people are government employees who won't get fired for standing up for themselves. I have also had bosses that I stood up to after I became a manager in private industry; they terminated me for standing up to them. But, again, I did not regret standing up to them when they tried to manipulate me and disrespect me and others. I cannot recommend challenging bad bosses unless you are able to accept being terminated or fired. I also do not recommend crossing the line to do something against your principles just because a bad manager tells you to do it. So, obviously, you will need to prepare and identify how far you will cross over the line before you just say no.

I was fortunate in my career because I was able to move on to another job whenever I found my current boss exhibiting disrespectful behavior. Not everyone is that fortunate. But my advice would be to be prepared by applying for other jobs that, if forced to, you could move to, to escape disrespect and emotionally immature behavior.

It is funny that my male friends used to kid me about "Who did you piss off now?" or "Try not to piss off your next boss." Not surprising that the male view would be that I was at fault. They could not relate to the fact that male managers act differently toward their female subordinates than their male subordinates. Any displeasure of a male boss would have to be the female employee's fault. I just laughed with them because they were my friends and I knew they could not relate. Meanwhile, I knew that the male managers with whom I could not relate had different views on emotional intelligence than I did and that I could not support them.

When I was the CIO for the Office of the Secretary in a large federal agency, I was in charge of the Help Desk. We had just switched over to a new e-mail system. The CFO, who was known to be a yeller and hard to get along with, sent an e-mail to the Help Desk asking how to bcc someone on an e-mail. The Help Desk representative did not know how to answer, so he told him that he would ask the vendor. That sent the CFO up the wall. He then e-mailed me to tell me that one of my Help Desk personnel didn't know how to do something he had asked about and had to ask the vendor. I went down to his office to give him personal attention. I stood outside his office and asked him, "Do you want me to show you how to bcc someone on an e-mail?" He started ranting and raving about the fact that the Help Desk didn't know how and had to ask the vendor, on and on. I asked him again, "Do you want me to show you how to bcc someone on an e-mail?" Again, more ranting and raving. Again, I asked, "Do you want me to show you how to bcc someone on an e-mail?" He gestured for me to come in. I showed him how to bcc someone in a second. He then started ranting and raving again. I tried to respond to his accusations that the Help Desk was learning, too, the best I could, given that he wouldn't stop ranting. I finally just left his office. The next thing I knew, my boss, the agency CIO, called me down to his office. He said that the CFO's secretary blamed me for upsetting the CFO. She said that, after I had been there, he went around the rest of the day and was angry and mean to everyone he encountered, including her. I said, "That's preposterous! I am not responsible for the CFO's bad behavior! He needs to take responsibility for his own behavior!" I was incredulous that I was being accused of the CFO's bad behavior when, to me, it seemed the norm rather than the exception. The CFO had no tolerance for people who could not or did not give him what he wanted immediately. This was emotional immaturity. At the CIO's direction, thereafter, I avoided the CFO and sent the most knowledgeable Help Desk representative if he had an IT issue. So much for mutual understanding.

Courage combats mediocrity in the workplace.

At any one time in my career, I could have given up and tried not to piss off my boss. I have seen many federal employees that have done just that. They stopped trying. They got beaten down so often that they had enough and just tried to survive in a toxic environment. They stayed in one position in the same organization for many years. Eventually, they learned that doing as little as possible did not attract attention, and they did not piss anyone off. With many people in an office practicing this safe behavior, mediocrity is the result. No one excels and shows anyone else up. Everyone makes mistakes, but they are seldom caught or corrected. Gradually, this becomes the culture of the office. Have you heard the expression that "10 percent of the people do 90 percent of the work?" That's what happens in an environment like the one I just described. Only 10 percent of the people have courage and motivation to be visible and excel outside the norm.

Another thing that happens in this type of culture is that people do not report managers' indiscretions. First of all, no one in their management chain cares or wants to hear such reports. If they are presented with a report that one of their managers has done something unethical, they cover it up in some way. That is something top management doesn't want to take time to deal with. There are no consequences for managers who misbehave. So people feel that reporting their manager's bad behavior is useless. Second, if you report a manager for something unethical, suddenly the person who submitted the report is highly visible. If there is an investigation, then the person has to prove, in some way, that the report is accurate. Sometimes it becomes "his word against mine." Also, reporting a manager means that you had to skip a layer in the management chain. This is viewed unfavorably by males, especially those who come from the military. Somehow, the person who submitted the report becomes the bad guy and goes through stressful times until the investigation is completed and a decision made. A classic example of this is the Catholic priests who were molesting young children. Such cases were covered up for years by the Catholic Church, and there were no consequences for the offenders. When report after report was made public, some of the offenders were finally brought to justice. People became aware that it was okay to report an offense; they would be safe, and the offender would suffer the consequences. It is true that there is safety in numbers. Look what happened in the case of Bill Cosby. One brave soul came forward and broke the ice. Then others got the courage to come forward. This is also true of the "Me, too" movement. Several television and movie personalities were held responsible for their abusive behavior to several or many women.

I admire my friend Lauren's courage. She is an educated, outspoken, able African American woman. She has had many jobs in her life in different disciplines. But because of that, she has a hard time finding a job in any one area. She hangs in there during times of unemployment and does not cry or whine. She just keeps applying for jobs. She never stops learning and growing. During times of unemployment, she finds courses in subjects she is interested in and gets certified in them, widening her knowledge and skills. She is determined to be her own person and be independent as much as she can. She is also determined to be her own boss one day and have her own business; she often brainstorms what kind of business she could start. I find that she sometimes demeans herself. I tell her that she can do anything she wants to do. She is a strong person with high principles and values. I admire the fact that she is always upbeat in spite of the fact that she has had some trying times finding jobs and having enough money to pay her bills.

I also admire my friend Mary's courage. It took courage to divorce her alcoholic, drug-user husband of sixteen years. It took courage to get a college education in her forties and go into debt doing so. It took courage to leave her small-town, redneck environment in South Carolina to come to Washington D.C. to get a job. It took courage to see a psychologist for four years to help her overcome her PTSD behavior developed from living with alcoholics (parents and husband) who physically and mentally abused her. When she got caught in a toxic work environment in a federal office, she kept a positive, upbeat attitude and found work immediately when her company terminated her. Fifteen years ago, she was in a bad accident in which a young man rammed her car in the rear at full speed as she was waiting to make a left turn. She had been in pain much of the time since then. It finally got so bad that she agreed to back surgery, not knowing what the results would be. She came through very well and was a model patient.

Both of these friends are sort of misfits in the big-city environment of Washington D.C. Yet, still, they exhibit courage to be who they are and not let the negative aspects of our culture keep them down. They exemplify the aspects of emotional intelligence and treat others with love and respect. They are motivated to be the best they can be and to keep learning and growing. (By the way, both of them are heavy users of the Internet to find things they want to know about and to learn).

Discipline

In order to become motivated to improve ourselves and our outlooks, we need to be disciplined. Discipline is what enables us to do what we need to do when we need to do it. It enables us to set and meet life goals. It enables us to control our emotions and the words coming out of our mouths. It enables us to listen to someone who is talking to us without interrupting and without judging what s/he is saying. It enables us to control our thoughts, as in meditation, and refuse to listen to bad or unhelpful tapes in our mind. In *Everyday Grace*, Marianne Williamson said, "Our greatest weakness is the weakness of an undisciplined mind."

My friend Kurt and I had an argument about discipline early on in our relationship. He argued that discipline was not necessary. I argued that it was. He was raised pretty much without discipline. His mother was an intellect and scientist. Back in her day, men were favored over women. She pretty much let her boys do whatever as they were growing up. Her first and last children, however, were girls. Her oversight over them was not well received by them. I, on the hand, was raised in the traditional German household where discipline is a way of life. I believe discipline is what got me through a tough curriculum in school (engineering). I believe discipline is what enables me to read book after book on self-help and work to apply the things I learned. I believe that discipline enables me to go to work every day on time and hardly ever take a sick day. In other words, discipline always motivates me to focus on the task at hand.

People I have known who are strangers to discipline create problems for themselves. For example, my friend Kurt was forever losing his keys. Whenever we went somewhere, he would spend at least fifteen minutes looking for his keys and cursing himself because he couldn't find them. I placed a basket near the door and told him that, whenever he came in the door, he was to place his keys in the basket. Then he would always know where they were when he went somewhere. It was hit or miss whether he did that or not. He didn't have the discipline to create a habit for himself that would enable him to be kind to himself. I've seen other people do things over and over that did not serve them. Another of my friends always had trash all over her car. Whenever she drove me somewhere, she would have to clean off the seat, and I would have to put my feet on the remainder of the stuff she didn't throw in the backseat. Putting a trash can on the seat for trash and emptying the trash once a week would take discipline and a few minutes of time and work.

Creating Healthy Habits

Emotional intelligence is creating helpful habits for yourself. As humans, creating healthy habits is how we train ourselves to do good things. I remember my mother saying, "You can train a child like you do a dog." She was talking about habits. When you tell a dog to sit, he sits and you give him a treat. When you teach a child to create a routine for himself, like brushing his teeth every night before bed, you get him in a good habit that benefits him with fewer cavities and trips to the dentist. So when you want to help yourself or others, create a habit of doing something that will become automatic and will please you.

I use the technique of creating habits in my work world, too. When I start a job, I set up routine times and places for meetings that will enable me to communicate with the people I need to communicate with. I also provide my staff with an operations manual that informs my staff what the routines of the job are. They don't have to guess or ask someone else; they can read and apply the routines themselves. When everyone knows what to expect on a daily basis, it makes things much easier day to day.

It takes discipline to meditate, especially if you meditate on a daily basis. You must set aside a time each day where you can separate yourself from the fierce activities of the day. It is easy to find excuses why you can't meditate any or every day. Maybe you just want to sit quietly for five minutes each morning. Nevertheless, whatever you do to center yourself and your emotions takes discipline.

The prophets Abraham, Jesus, Muhammad, and Buddha all had discipline. They used discipline to focus on their spiritual convictions and lead others on their spiritual paths. Meditation requires discipline. Meditation is controlling our thoughts or stream of consciousness. Emotional intelligence requires invoking reason in response to external stimuli and discipline in controlling our resulting thoughts and emotional reactions. It takes discipline to learn and apply the tools for emotional intelligence and keep practicing them.

Communication

As a manager, I learned that all problems in the workplace stem from communication: lack of communication, misunderstood communication or miscommunication, too much communication whereby the receiver stops digesting, or just plain bad communication whereby the sender incites negative emotions in the receiver. Leaders have to be ace communicators to understand the people they are leading and to get their message across. Lone wolves or people with emotional problems are known for their antisocial behaviors and have difficulty communicating with others.

When I first became a manager, what hit me hardest was the need to communicate continually during the workday. People were constantly coming in to my office to ask me what to do about this and about that. If they presented me with a problem, I had to seek out other people to find resolutions to the problems. There were constant meetings, presentations, and briefings. Being an introvert, by the end of the day I was exhausted and just wanted to go home and be alone. I soon realized that, once I stepped into the office, I was role-playing. I was suddenly an extrovert with good listening skills. I learned that there is no accomplishing work and resolving issues unless you constantly communicate. Now, when I start a new job as a manager, I immediately start a dialogue with my employees, with my customer, and with my company. I set up methods and times of regular communication with them. I develop a communication plan for all to follow. The plan includes rules for communicating.

Communication is our method of learning about others to understand them. Daniel Goleman says in his book *Working with Emotional Intelligence*:

> "Being an adept communicator is the keystone of all social skills. Among managers, communications competence

133

strongly distinguishes star performers from average or poor ones; the lack of this ability…can torpedo morale.

Listening well, the key to empathy, is also crucial to competence in communicating. Listening skills—asking astute questions, being open-minded and understanding, not interrupting, seeking suggestions—account for about a third of people's evaluations of whether someone they work with is an effective communicator.

Being in control of our own moods is also essential to good communication…In dealing with peers and subordinates, calmness and patience were key."

Notice Goleman says "being in control of our own moods." How do we do this? I offer several different means in subsequent sections. But the main thing is to acknowledge and understand your feelings at any one time and then manage them using the techniques of meditation, talking to a friend or confident, writing in a journal, writing yourself a letter, and so on.

In *Think Again*, Adam Grant says:

"Listening well is more than a matter of talking less. It's a set of skills in asking and responding. It starts with showing more interest in other people's interests rather than trying to judge their status or prove our own."

Eliminate hurtful words and judgment from your communication.

When we are emotionally intelligent, we eliminate hurtful words and judgment from our communication. We care to find out what the best methods of communication are and implement them. We sense when the receiver is open or closed to our output. We do not filter input but process it carefully and completely. Instead we filter our output, eliminating words that could be hurtful or misunderstood. We cannot expect to effectively communicate with someone whom we approach with blame and judgment.

Have you ever noticed that, nine times out of ten, when someone posts something on Facebook (or Twitter), no matter how innocuous the post may be, someone will have something negative to say about it, sometimes even hurtful? "Everyone is a critic!" Why can't we just share our happiness?

The best thing to do is to ignore the negative comments, no matter how difficult that may be.

Someone recently started a discussion on the Facebook page of my neighborhood group about the noise the Navy helicopters were making as they flew overhead. I responded to a woman who said it sounded like they were going to land in her backyard. This was the conversation:

> Her: It sounded like a helicopter was going to land in my yard.
> Me: Really
> Her: Really, really. My windows shook as they flew over.
> Me: I take it as an honor that they chose to fly over my house. You?
> Her: I don't look at it as personal. I see it as a nuisance.
> Me: That's one way to look at it.
> Her: I don't even know who you are and yet you seem to have a problem with me.
> Me: (nothing)

Despite the fact that I agreed with her and accepted her responses, she misinterpreted my words as an attack. I couldn't figure out why. I didn't respond to her last remark. I had a feeling she didn't get my "really." It's possible that it's a generational thing. My friends and I were always saying "really" to confirm what the other person had just said. She may have been younger, and she and her friends do not use the expression in the same way. She may have interpreted my words as doubting or questioning her.

One day, I exited the Metro train and headed down the escalator. In front of me, an African American man stood in the center of the escalator stair holding up a line of people who wanted to walk down the escalator to the left. An African American woman came up behind me and said, "If you want to stand you have to move to the right." The man immediately moved to the right and traffic continued down the escalator on the left. I was in awe. I can't tell you how many times I've seen someone block the escalator by standing on the left so that no one could walk down the stairs. No one says anything. They just stand there and wait. I'm one of those.

But here is a woman whose communication was very effective. She merely stated the facts and all were served. I said to myself, *I want to be like her!*

We all know that communication can make or break a relationship and a marriage. Lack of communication or deception easily leads to a breakup. Sometimes the words we choose to express ourselves are not well received and have a negative effect on the receiver or even the relationship. Sometimes the truth hurts and we just have to lay it out there. Daniel Goleman says in his book *Working with Emotional Intelligence* that successful marriages are those where both partners "show each other that they are being listened to." He says:

> "The presence or absence of ways to repair a rift is a crucial difference between the fights of couples who have a healthy marriage and those of couples who eventually end up divorcing…One overall strategy for making a marriage work is not to concentrate on specific issues—childrearing, sex, money, housework—that couples fight about, but rather to cultivate a couple's shared emotional intelligence, thereby improving the chances of working things out. A handful of emotional competencies—mainly being able to calm down (and calm your partner), empathy, and listening well—can make it more likely a couple will settle their disagreements effectively."

Understand that there are gender and cultural differences in communication.

Emotional intelligence means that we understand there are gender and cultural differences in communication. There were many times as a woman working in a male-dominated organization I was outnumbered and not listened to. I often wondered, *Did I not make myself clear?* I eventually learned that my male counterparts just had filters, and although I was clear in what I said, they did not *hear* what I said. I can still picture a meeting in an Office Director's (male) office with several other men. We were there to discuss and resolve an issue. I said, "Why don't we …" The Office Director said emphatically, "No!" So I stopped speaking. It wasn't but a few minutes later that one of the men said the exact same thing in slightly different words. The Office Director said, "That's a good idea." I was shocked. I thought, *Isn't that what I said? Wasn't I clear?* Now I understand why that happens.

When I was a CIO in the Office of the Secretary in a large federal agency, I supervised four African American women. I thought I was being friendly and often used the term "the gals" to speak of the women I supervised. One of them called it to my attention that she didn't like to be called "a gal" because women slaves were often called "gals." I thought that that was such a long time ago and thought we should have moved past that, but I, nonetheless, respected her request, understanding that she came from a different culture and viewpoint than I.

There are entire books on communicating and communications. I've read several that are very good. Deborah Tannen wrote two books I read that helped me: *You Just Don't Understand* and *That's Not What I Meant.* I've taken leadership courses where we were trained in active listening: listen, digest, then summarize and provide feedback. So, communicating well takes knowledge and practice and sometimes just hard work.

Understanding/Awareness

Understanding means taking the time to get to know ourselves or others and what makes us/them tick. This, of course, includes work and time and excludes assumptions and presumptions—presumptions as in biases and prejudices we learned from either our past experiences or from other people. It requires active listening (i.e., asking the right questions and processing the answers) and observing body language. Body language should match verbal communication, or something is not consistent. If it is not consistent, we begin to suspect something deeper and underlying that the verbal communication is not conveying.

Having a mentor or professional listener can be helpful.

To understand ourselves and improve our emotional outlooks, some of us see a therapist, counselor, psychologist, psychiatrist, or spiritual director. Some of us just talk with a friend or confidante we know we can trust. Some of us read self-help books and see things we can relate to. We all need help sometimes whether we acknowledge it or not. If we don't have a friend and confidante to help us to understand ourselves, there are professionals trained to help us learn more about ourselves and grow. When it comes down to it, these people are professional listeners. In the end, though, it is we who have to choose our paths; it is we who have to make decisions for ourselves based on our understanding. But there is value in having someone listen to us, even if we have to pay them to do so. Sometimes we can't believe what we are saying when we say it out loud to someone. It may be something we never admitted to ourselves. It makes a difference when someone makes an effort to listen to us without judgment. In addition, these trained people can suggest tools and techniques if and when we encounter certain situations. These suggestions can provide us with a different outlook and widen our viewpoints of ourselves and others. This is an example of benefiting from a trained professional and growing.

Understanding others is not an easy matter. I realized this in conversations with my friend Lauren. She asked me to go with her to her monthly Buddhist meeting in the morning. Afterwards, she tried to help me in my search for what to do next in my life—do I continue to pursue a job as a Program Manager, or do I do something entirely different. She told me that I need to create what I want to do next. I indicated that I didn't know what else I could do because I had found a job I would like and had been picturing myself going there every day and enjoying it, you know, trying to manifest it. She told me that I had been giving off negative energy in my past jobs and that is why I was terminated. I think that may have been the case, but I didn't go into the jobs with negative energy. At each place I worked during the past two years, there was someone there who had a personal agenda that I could not buy into. It's not like I decided one day that I didn't belong and started giving off negative vibes. I think that, in explaining to Lauren why each job ended, I oversimplified things and just picked something, one thing, to explain. Therefore, she was able to zero in on one problem and one solution. I checked in with myself and was open to her suggestions. But the solution is not as easy as she suggested. I think I actually had been doing what she suggested. At each place I worked in the past couple years, there was a long sequence of events that led up to my termination or my resignation. There was one theme, though, in each case. Someone at each place I worked had a personal agenda that they were determined to execute that was different from the one I was working under. While I believed that we all had the same agenda—the mission of the organization and/or the statement of work in the contract, we did not. I was not privy to their agenda, and that was on purpose. I only realized their agenda as events unfolded. In the meantime, unbeknownst to me, I kept getting in their way and had to be eliminated. I never fully related the entire scenario to any of my friends because it would take too long and would be too boring for them. From Lauren's and my discussion today, I realized that she was missing a lot of information that I had. That's what made me realize how difficult it is to understand someone else and what they are going through. It's never black and white. There is so much more than we will ever know that goes into their thinking and their behavior. There is so much more to a situation or event in someone's life than we will likely know. This is the reason we should not judge others. As much as we try to understand, we can never know and understand their entire being. This is why it is hard to give people advice. The person we are advising may know so much more than we do. We can only open ourselves up, listen to what others tell us, and try to understand on a level that we can at the moment. We may find later, as we get to know them better or events unfold through time, that we can understand what they were talking about at an even deeper level. And we may find out that our deductions in the past were inaccurate and so was our advice. When communicating with someone else about ourselves, we can't expect them to understand all that we are thinking and feeling. They can only understand the information we provide them. If we leave out relevant history or past feelings, they will only understand what we tell them in the present.

Find a person in the workplace who will support/mentor you.

Wherever you work, you will find people with their own agendas, but you will also find people who are helpful to others. It is a good practice to find someone in the workplace who will support/mentor you. While I was Chief of Staff to the CIO of a large federal agency, my boss, the CIO, had a secretary named Mindy. He was "stuck" with Mindy, who was African American, because none of the other white male managers wanted her. Mindy was very vocal about what she wanted and what she would and would not do. She was cantankerous most of the time, and everyone tried to avoid her. As the CIO's Chief of Staff, I felt it was my duty to provide him with the best support I could. So I started talking with Mindy on a personal level. I got her to open up about why she was so belligerent most of the time. She said she felt that she and the other blacks downtown were getting "screwed over" by the white managers. So she refused to be "used" by them. I explained to her that she was in a high-paying secretarial job and that she needed to perform in a professional manner for her boss's sake. I assured her that I would help her. She actually turned around, and her new attitude was visible. She was more friendly and accepting. She took on new tasks without an argument. She tried to reduce the number of errors in her writing and be more professional. But when I left that job and the

CIO appointed me as the CIO of the Office of the Secretary with my own secretary, Mindy resorted back to her previous cantankerous behavior. It was disappointing to see. No one else tried to work with her and support her like I did. No one took on that job. Her bitterness again showed through. It was hard for me to watch her revert back to her belligerent behavior.

I could never fully understand why Mindy behaved the way she did. I did not witness or experience all the treatment or mistreatment she experienced in her past. I could only understand what she told me as the explanation of why she behaved in the manner she did. The fact is Mindy did respond to my trying to understand her views and support her to succeed. The English in her e-mails was poor, but we worked together to improve her writing. I reviewed the e-mails she sent for wider distribution, and she learned from it. She felt better about herself and her contribution to the CIO's success, all because someone tried to understand her and support her. It was a deeper understanding than that of just her views. As Daniel Goleman said in *Working with Emotional Intelligence*: "The resolution requires that each side be able to understand not just the other's point of view, but their needs and fears." I understood Mindy's need to feel valued and her fear of being disrespected. She understood my need for providing the CIO with quality service and my fear of her disgracing or discrediting his office if she continued her belligerent attitude.

Learn about the cultural differences of coworkers.

The workplace is a perfect opportunity to learn and understand cultural differences. One thing my friendship with Lauren has done for me is to help me understand the African American perspective. I hired Lauren when I was a Program Manager on a three-year contract. Lauren was my Program Coordinator. She is African American. She stands out as a person. She has a strong and sturdy body and is nice looking. She likes to wear her hair in different ways different weeks. She is very well spoken and once was a member of Toastmasters, a group of people who write and present speeches for each other to critique to become better speakers. Lauren is a capable person who believes in doing things well. She is friendly and open and is well-liked. When she came on board, I made room for her in my own cubicle so that we could back each other up and continually exchange information. In down times, we started talking about our personal lives. We were impressed with each other that we both had grown up in St. Louis, Missouri, we both were spiritual, and we both loved and had cats. But in addition to that, she introduced me to what it was like being black in our society. She told me how if she was pulled over by the police in her car, she immediately put both hands up on the steering wheel so that the cop would know she wasn't reaching for a weapon. I was shocked! I never had to think of something like that. She taught me some words that were in her vocabulary but not in mine. When incidents occurred that involved whites versus blacks, she would explain her reaction to the incident in terms of a black person. We would even laugh about differences in our experiences and viewpoints as black and white people. Recently, I arrived at her house to help her de-clutter her lower level. She had just come outside to walk her dog. She immediately handed me the leash so I could walk the dog instead. She said, "This is a case of *The Help* in reverse." I said, "Right. I thought about that when I came to your house to work on your landscape and you weren't home. I figured the (predominantly black) neighborhood would be interested to know you had a white landscaper." Lauren is the first black person I was ever close to. It opened my eyes to how open, unthreatened dialogue between people of different races could easily eliminate biases and change old viewpoints based on hearsay. Lauren caused me to be conscious of the black viewpoint and the disparity between how blacks and whites are treated in our society. And I am grateful for her gift to me.

Lauren was the second Program Coordinator I hired in that position. The first woman was also African American. We found a desk for the first woman in a cubicle on the floor below ours since my Deputy and I were in the same cubicle when she was hired. As time went on, I found that the Program Coordinator spent most of her time on her cell phone, listening to music, and ignoring e-mail requests for work to be done. I told her that I wanted her to move into my cube so that we could exchange information and develop a good working relationship. That just wasn't happening when she was on a different floor. Before I could have her desk moved, though, the company HR person recommended that I terminate her for lying and saying she did not receive an e-mail request I sent her. (The IT guy verified she received it). I terminated her in the usual way, saying that we no longer needed her services and escorted her to the door. The next day, I received an e-mail from her saying that she was not my slave—slavery was over—and I had better mend my ways as a tyrant manager, and on and on. I did not respond because I didn't want to fuel the negativity. I knew she would be angry at me for terminating her. If anything, I erred on the lenient side for too long. Her anger could have worked to her detriment if I were to mention it to future potential employers calling past supervisors for references. How different was Lauren's behavior when I explained I wanted her to sit in my cubicle so we could exchange information. That's what she wanted, too! The first person was more concerned with her personal agenda of talking to her friends on the phone and playing her music during the day than she was concerned with her responsibilities and the work that needed to be done.

There were many times in my career that I complained about my boss's behavior to my male friends or my husband. It was clear to me that my boss was treating me differently from his male subordinates, and adversely, in fact. But my male friends or husband would discount my stories and somehow find blame with me for the behavior. I came to realize that, since men have no experience being a woman, they could not possibly understand what I was encountering and feeling in the stories I related. They could not relate. Sexism was a totally foreign experience for them and not even on their radar screen.

I have read many books that helped me understand other spiritual philosophies, other religions, the other gender, on and on. When I started dating a man with a mental illness, I read about depression and men with depression. As a manager, I read books to understand human behavior. The titles of these books are in my list of books I read in the appendix. One of my favorites was *The Gender Knot* by Allan Johnson. His descriptions of gender differences were so well worded and nonjudgmental.

Understanding goes hand-in-hand with awareness. Awareness brings us opportunities to understand the situation and what we should do. We must continually be aware of our surroundings and the people surrounding us. We must continually be aware of who we are and how we should relate to our surroundings. We must continually be aware of opportunities to make a difference for others. In *Everyday Grace*, Marianne Williamson said, "The attention we pay to the nature of our thinking...is the most powerful attention we can pay."

Learn and understand personality types

There are many different personality tests to take today to better understand yourself and others. The Myers-Briggs test has been very popular and lasted the test of time. It is often used in federal organizations and companies for managers to understand their staff and vice versa. The assumption of the Myers-Briggs Type Indicator (MBTI) is that each of us is born with a preference for four of the eight personality traits that the MBTI measures. These preferences can change during your lifetime and in different situations. For example, in my early professional life, I tested at the extreme edges of an "ISTJ"—Introvert, Sensor, Thinker, Judger (meaning I *strongly* preferred those traits). After I had been a manager for a while, I took a Myers-Briggs type test for preferences at work. I tested as an "ENFP"—Extrovert, Intuiter, Feeler, Perceiver. I found that, as a manager, I had to learn and practice communicating and responding to the needs of other people all day long. I found myself taking on the role of a manager, as an actor would take on the role of a character on stage, when I found my way to my desk at work each morning. When I went home, I found I could relax and assume my innate preferences to regain my energy by being alone and thinking about what had happened that day—what I did well and what I could have done better.

The Enneagram has become popular lately. My best friend from high school recommended I read the book *The Enneagram Made Easy* to better understand myself and why I behave the way I do. The Enneagram is a study of the nine basic types of people. The roots of the Enneagram go back many centuries; it arrived in the U.S. in the 1960s. The book states up front that it is best that each person discover their own type(s) by completing the exercises in the beginning of each chapter. It cautions against "typing" other people yourself and making assumptions. I found that I had characteristics in most of the nine types but more so in two or three. Immediately, I found that it explained my behavior and reactions to a communication exchange I had with a friend after I had finished reading the book.

When I was an Acquisition Manager in the federal government dealing with a difficult Program Manager, the government offered us a mediation session as part of the EEO Office's Alternative Dispute Resolution

Program. During an all-day session, we both took several personality type tests. One was the Strength Deployment Inventory which is based on seven motivational value systems. It provided us our "Conflict Sequences" to show us how we responded when faced with conflict and opposition. Another was the Thomas-Kilmann Conflict Mode Instrument which is designed to assess an individual's behavior in conflict situations. The test results and how they fit both our personalities were fascinating. The results helped me understand that it was easy for us to be at odds—we had very different personalities and personal objectives/motivations. We did learn something new about each other. After the mediation session was over and we returned to work, however, the mean-spirited treatment I received from the Program Manager and the Contracting Officer continued (because, I believe, it was driven by a motive other than not understanding our differences).

During leadership training throughout my career, some of the tests I took included:

- Emotional Quotient Inventory (EQI)—helps you better understand your emotional and social functioning
- FIRO-B (Fundamental Interpersonal Relations Orientation-Behavior)—measures how you tend to behave with others and what you seek from them
- Leader Behavior Analysis II Self-A (LBAII)—provides you with information about your perceptions of your own leadership style
- The Personal Profile System—presents a plan to help you understand self and others in a specific environment. The results are provided in a graph of the DISC Dimensions of Behavior: Dominance, Influence, Steadiness, and Conscientiousness
- The Parker Team Player Survey—identifies your style as a team player.

Never assume and never stop learning about others

My friend Lauren called me to tell me she had been contacted by a recruiter from a large, popular company to fill a position with a big title. She said that this time (as opposed to other times when she freaked out when she had been approached by a recruiter for a position with an impressive title), she was going to work on her self-confidence. I had gently been telling her for years that she too readily demeans herself and her abilities. When I was her supervisor, I continually encouraged her to step outside her comfort zone and use her otherwise unused skills. Recently, she explained that if she felt she didn't have the knowledge to do something right, she was reluctant to do it. I applaud her for being cautious about that because I have seen too many people in job positions they couldn't handle. She told me that the recruiter asked her if she had experience writing policies. She couldn't think of any right away and asked the recruiter if she would be developing new policies or improving existing ones. The recruiter responded that that was a good question and that she didn't know the answer; she would have to ask her management. Meanwhile, Lauren was panicking to come up with something she did that would count as experience writing policies. She said the low self-esteem tapes started playing. I said, "There you go again!" She said, "Now that just isn't helpful. I am working on my self-esteem, but I have to deal with the demeaning messages I received from my environment all my life." (As an educated African American in a big city, she has experienced discrimination both subtle and outright). I appreciated her telling me that what I said did not help. That way I could refrain from saying things in the future that did not serve her well. I mentioned that a difference between us (and there are so many likenesses) is that my mother thought I was the best person on earth and would always tell me how smart and capable I was (in between her telling me what to do and what not to do). Lauren didn't have that experience in her adult life. Lauren acknowledged how having a family member bolster your self-esteem would help. She told me that she took deep breaths to calm herself and finally realized that the *Operations Manual* she had developed when she worked for me was really a policy and procedure document. I agreed! We were both so happy! I felt honored that Lauren chose to call me and share her triumph with me.

Love/Compassion/Empathy

Marianne Williamson said in her book *Return to Love*: "Love is what we were born with. Fear is what we have learned here. The spiritual journey is the relinquishment—or unlearning—of fear and the acceptance of love back into our hearts." She says: "Every problem, inside and out, is due to separation from love on someone's part."

Self-love must come first.

Before loving others, we must first love ourselves. If we love ourselves, then loving others is just our "cup runneth over." I'm not talking about lusting over someone where the passion is great for the first year or so and then there is nothing. I'm talking about loving someone where there is hard work done to understand, admire, accept, and respect someone. I see the steps to loving oneself as first to rid ourselves of any bad tapes we are constantly playing from childhood such as, "You're not good enough," "You're lazy," "You're stupid," and on and on. Sometimes, in childhood, our parents say things to us to try to motivate us, but the words hurt us instead and have a negative effect on us. The second step is for us to work on small habits that are harmful to ourselves. For example, if you think you make too many mistakes whenever you do something, start slowing down and taking your time to do things more carefully. Of course, this is easier said than done. Changing something takes setting small goals and practicing. I didn't say, "If you think you are overweight, then try losing weight." I would say the majority of us think we are overweight. There are so many factors that determine our weight—genes, learned eating patterns, body hormones, illnesses, appropriate medications, and so on. So I won't address that here. The key here is to address behavior that is hurtful to yourself and others. Sometimes it is best to seek help from professionals to change or eliminate harmful behavior or habits.

One thing I had to do when Kurt and I broke up was to start doing things for myself. That's when I bought my house in Annapolis. I learned to like Annapolis and liked being by the water when I stayed with Kurt in Annapolis on the weekends. I decided I didn't need him for me to live in Annapolis. So I bought a house there. I can safely say that that is one of the best things I did for myself to feed my soul (besides buying a little red 300ZX when I was in my thirties). It is a weekend escape from the hustle and bustle of the big city, Washington D.C. Also, Kurt used to make candlelight dinners for himself. I thought to myself, *I should do that!* Now I do that regularly. The lighted candles are a sign that I love myself and am taking care of myself. I had to decide what I liked to do and do it. That was not easy. I took the year we broke up to try different things and decide which things were most important to me. I still have to ask myself frequently, "What do I want to do?" I open myself to signs from the Universe of what it wants me to do—people I meet who can guide me, circumstances that point to a certain activity that is right at the time, and so on. I feel that the Universe created circumstances for me to be able to take time to write this book. I have faith that the Universe will also present opportunities for me to share my book with others and use it to teach and mentor others.

Love and respect go hand in hand. If you don't respect someone, it is hard to love them. I have had many bosses whose behavior I could not condone. I lost respect for them. I knew, then, that I had to change jobs, or else I would risk doing or saying something that would not serve the relationship. I have also had bosses who I admired for their skills and their respect for other people. I saw them as role models. My personal relationships are based on mutual respect. When someone respects me and others, I am willing to return the favor and continue the relationship. If someone does not respect me or others, I lose my respect for him/her. They soon got the picture, and one of us ends the relationship.

When we lose respect for someone, we have to try to understand why they are behaving in the way they are behaving. Usually they are fearful of something. We have to use this understanding to elevate our feelings toward them to one of a general love for all—all who have human flaws and are fearful of something. On a higher level, we know that we will never be able to totally understand what that person has experienced in his/her life and what his/her motivation is. We need to use emotional intelligence to take the high road and prevent any destructive emotions or our ego from dictating our behavior toward someone for whom we lose respect.

Taking care of your body is a must.

When you love yourself, you take care of your body. You feed it the nourishment it needs to be healthy and ward off disease. You listen to your body. If it feels different or something is happening that is unusual, check it out. One winter, every evening I would drink a glass of red wine at 5:00 p.m., happy hour. It would warm me up, relax me, and I had something to look forward to every day. By the end of the winter, though, I noticed I was having diarrhea every morning and had a rash on both sides of my face close to the hairline. I looked up allergies to red wine on the Internet, and, sure enough, I had the symptoms of an allergy to the tannic acid in red wine. When I stopped drinking red wine, the symptoms went away. That was disappointing! Now I have to substitute something else like warm tea on those cold winter evenings. There are books on how keeping your body free from toxins can keep you from getting cancer or cure it. Marilu Henner and her husband, Michael Brown, wrote a book on how Marilu helped Michael lick cancer by ridding his body of toxins and preparing food for him that helped his body heal. We all know that smoking causes cancer. Starting to smoke means that you signed up for cancer and an early death. Stress causes disease. There are entire books on listening to your body, managing weight, and exercising to keep it fit. Exercise not only nourishes the body, it is good for the body and soul. The result of taking care of your body is that you are doing your part to keep a healthy balance of mind, body, and soul.

Public Radio featured a story on the increase of adolescent eating disorders during the pandemic. The guest doctor called the pandemic the "perfect storm for adolescent eating disorders." A fifteen-year-old told her story of how the feeling of isolation, trauma, and having no control over her life caused her downward spiral from an eating disorder and eventual hospitalization due to malnourishment. Her growth and development were stunted during that period. Her mother found that there was a shortage of therapists who could treat her daughter, there were so many cases. They eventually placed her in a hospital designed to treat patients with mental health issues. This is what finally pulled her through that rough period in her life. This is a perfect example of the tight link between our emotions and physical health. If one is in danger, so is the other.

Have compassion for others.

If you try to understand a person and why they behave the way they do, this is the first step to compassion. Much of the time, we can relate to something in another's life's experiences that influenced them, and we can empathize with them. Even if we haven't had similar experiences as the other person, we can put ourselves in their position and imagine how we would feel.

Erich Fromm defines "love" in his book *Sane Society*:

> "Productive love always implies a syndrome of attitudes; that of care, responsibility, respect, and knowledge. If I love, I care—that is, I am actively concerned with the other person's growth and happiness…I am responsible, that is, I respond to his needs…I respect him, that is, I look at him as he is, objectively and not distorted by my wishes and fears. I know him, I have penetrated through his surface to the core of his being and related myself to him from my core."

Daniel Goleman says in his book *Working with Emotional Intelligence*:

> "Empathy is essential as an emotional guidance system, piloting us in getting along at work. Beyond mere survival, empathy is critical for superior performance wherever the job focus is on people…Empathy is crucial to excellence."

Keep in mind that one of the side effects of antidepressants is a lack of empathy for others. I experienced this with two close friends. One of them was my friend Kurt. I did not know him before he was on Paxil. He was on Paxil the entire time we were in a relationship. One thing that showed up for me while we were in a relationship was his lack of empathy for me and my feelings. For example, I remember one time we were sitting on his front porch and I was pouring my heart out about something. Kurt saw a neighbor walking by, and right in the middle of my pouring my heart out, he ran outside and started talking to the neighbor. I was shocked and hurt. When he finally came back in, I told him he hurt my feelings. He showed little empathy and didn't seem to get why that hurt me.

When I researched the side effects of antidepressants, I found a blog on the subject. One young woman said she refused to take antidepressants because it would reduce her empathy for others. I thought, *How aware and bright is this woman!* So beware, if you need help getting through a period of depression, an antidepressant is a short-time help to get over the hump. Otherwise, it might alter and take over your personality. If possible, you want to understand your emotions and have the control to deal with them yourself.

People rise to the occasion with an outpouring of love when others need it. If you want examples of love and compassion, just look at the reactions of people to mass shootings. On June 12, 2016 a lone gunman went on a shooting spree in a popular gay nightclub in Orlando, Florida. He murdered forty-nine people and injured fifty-three, many very seriously. The mass shooting prompted an outpouring of sympathy across the globe, with people unfurling rainbow flags and holding vigils in tribute to the victims. After the shooting, Orlando's OneBlood donation center put a call out on Twitter saying there was an urgent need for plasma donors. So many people responded that the organization's website crashed and their voicemail box filled. Hundreds of people stood in line for hours at various blood donation centers in Florida. The response was overwhelming.

Buddhism teaches compassion for others. The Dalai Lama is all about compassion. Some of his many books are:

- *An Open Heart, Practicing Compassion in Everyday Life*
- *The Dalai Lama's Big Book of Happiness, How to Live in Freedom, Compassion, and Love*
- *How to be Compassionate, a Handbook for Creating Inner Peace in a Happier World*

Kathleen Kelly

I enjoyed reading the Dalai Lama's *An Open Heart*. In it the Dalai Lama said:

> "Compassion is the wish that the other be free of suffering...In the first step toward a compassionate heart, we must develop our empathy or closeness to others. We must also recognize the gravity of their misery. The closer we are to a person, the more unbearable we find that person's suffering."

Accepting Differences

After being a federal employee for thirty-five years and working for the federal government as a contractor for another thirteen years, I have concluded that there are a lot of emotionally immature people in the world. You get to know people pretty well spending eight to nine hours a day with them and doing things with them every day. I have had jerk bosses in both the government and in private industry. It seems that the persons who need help to grow are the last persons to seek the help. It always amazed me that, when the government offered training in such subjects as leadership, management, supervision, EEO, sexual harassment, and so on, the people who exemplified what was being taught were the people who attended the training. The training was just a confirmation that they were on the right track. After the training, we would go back to our work environment and have to deal with the people who did not take the training and who did not exemplify what was taught in the training. The training seemed to apply to a perfect world only.

So what is the answer? Acceptance. Acceptance that there are people in the world who are different from you, have different values, and, as a result, behave differently. Your reaction should depend on whether or not another person's behavior in the workplace is destructive to you. I learned that if your work situation is such that you are singled out and suppressed, the best answer is for you to leave that environment. Sure, chances are that you will encounter another difficult situation in a new job, but you can't give up hope. As both a federal employee and a contractor for the government, I have dealt with some pretty difficult people. Most of these people believed, *It's my way or the highway.* As I matured, I stopped trying to show them other ways of doing things or trying to work around them, which usually did not work anyway. I just learned to take the highway (as fast as I could).

A lesson in acceptance is getting to know people of different cultures, religions, and so on. My house in Silver Spring, Maryland, was in a well-established, predominantly Jewish neighborhood. My neighbors on one side were orthodox Jews. But my street was always diverse. In addition to Jewish families, we had African American, Greek, and Italian families. One house was owned by an older gay white man. Ownership is turning over, and younger people are moving in, buying from the original owners. More recently, a woman from Guyana moved into the cul de sac. There were several new Jewish families. For me, this was the perfect opportunity to learn about other ethnic groups and accept their different ways of living. Most of the people are busy living their own lives and don't spend much time outside or mingling with their neighbors. Neither neighbor on either side of me knew much about landscaping or yard maintenance. So I helped. I applied fertilizer and weed killer to my next-door neighbor's front yard for her. That way, I helped her out, and her weeds didn't migrate to my yard.

In Annapolis, my house is in a diverse neighborhood. Surrounding me are older, original Eastportoricans. Some of the old timers are tough and not so friendly. They are from a traditional blue-collar culture and worked hard all their lives. They stay to themselves in a small town where everyone else knows your business. On one side of me, two elderly women and one of the women's son live in a run-down house. Since I moved in, they have done absolutely no maintenance on the house. On the other side of me is a single white male who is "very cool" and creative. He has made modifications to his home to accommodate his lifestyle. On his back deck, he frequently entertains friends. The women next door do nothing to keep their yard up. They hire a man to mow the yard when it needs it, but he does nothing else. Therefore, weeds and invasive Bermuda grass creep into my yard. So, I maintain a swath along their side of the fence with weed killer and pull out the Bermuda grass. I've grown to accept and just deal with it. I accept that I am more anal about my yard and landscaping than most people. My being anal benefits both parties. It means more work for me, but I'm glad I can handle it. And it's the more relaxed, diverse atmosphere in Annapolis that appeals to me.

Down the street is "the hood." The hood is subsidized apartment housing and predominantly African American. During hot summer nights, you can hear loud music and shouting late into the night. Sometimes there is gunfire. Down the street the other way, is the "yuppie creep." Yuppies are buying and either renovating the original houses or tearing them down and building new houses. The yuppies have to be sure they lock everything up on their property, or else it will be gone. That's just the fact of life living there. One time I reported to the police a strange truck parked on my street that was there all day and overnight. At one point, there were three Latinos in the cab having a good time. That's what made me suspicious—why were they hanging out in the truck for so long? It turned out that the truck had been stolen from a man in another neighborhood. He had started it up and then went in the house to get something. When he came out again, it was gone.

Most of the emotionally immature people I encountered were control freaks. They each had their own method of controlling the situation or people. Most were intelligent in the respect that they manipulated the situation to get their way. But they did not or were not capable of reasoning things through for the good of all involved. They justified what they did in some way to make them and others believe they were doing the right thing for the mission. But most people were not fooled. It angered me when people lied to my face and talked down to me in order to justify what they were doing. Did they actually think that I would believe their lies? That didn't matter to them. They went on with their charade and were great actors. All the while I knew they were afraid of something—losing their job, being found out as an incompetent or a bad manager, and so on. But there was no way they would admit it or maybe even acknowledge it to themselves. I just wish they had been honest and said just once, "I'm not sure what to do in this case, but let's talk over our options to help me reach a reasonable decision." No, they always acted as if they were the only one who knew what to do and made a decision based on what little they knew about the subject, accurate or inaccurate. Not knowing something is not a weakness. Refusing to learn is.

Recently, I was a contractor and managed a task of seven contractors that prepared security documentation for a federal office that was sent to the CIO's office for review and approval. A briefing was prepared after the review of the documentation for presentation to the system managers and CIO for authorization to operate each federal system. The (federal) Branch Chief was bright and knew his security stuff. But he was a bad manager. Our team was dealt surprise (earlier) deadlines, continual new (unplanned) and different work, lack of review or feedback from the government, and so on. No matter how hard we planned and tried to get ahead of the game, we failed (in the government's eyes). The Branch Chief continually berated every member of my team. Every daily meeting I had with him in the morning turned into a rant about at least one team member. It was exasperating. We always did what the government representatives asked us to do. One day, my team and I requested a meeting with the Branch Chief to go over documentation that we had prepared but had received no feedback or direction on. Instead of providing the review we needed (because he had not even looked at the documentation we had prepared), the Branch Chief ranted on and on about how we weren't doing our job and produced garbage. I tried desperately to keep cool and focus him on what we needed from him. He then ordered everyone out of the room except my Deputy and me. I told him that we had delivered what he had requested within the time allotted. I told him that he was not providing us the feedback we needed in a timely manner, and, therefore, we ended up in these situations where he accused us of not doing our job when he hadn't even reviewed what we produced. He finally got my view. He said, "Then you think that you did your job and I am at fault." I said, "Yes." He told me he disagreed but that he understood what I was saying, and the meeting ended. The next thing that happened was that I received an e-mail from him telling me that I acted unprofessionally at the meeting, sighing and rolling my eyes when he was talking, and that I basically needed to clean up my act. I was livid! Even if I had done what he described, he was taking no responsibility for my exasperation. I knew from working for the same organization for thirty years what this was. He was on the defensive because I stood up to him and pointed out his responsibility. At the meeting, he saw nothing that he could or would change to make things better. So he sent me an e-mail degrading my professional reputation and bcc'd upper-level managers in his chain, one of which was a good friend of mine. This is the old "destroy her reputation before people think it is me" routine. I did not respond to that e-mail. I also learned that if you respond to e-mails like that, you only get in deeper. The routine is that your response is also forwarded to the people he originally bcc'd. He came to my cube later that day and said that we should meet for coffee and talk things through. I was cool and calm and let him do all the talking. He told me that he didn't bcc anyone on that e-mail (which I did not ask him). I knew he was lying on both accounts. We never met for coffee, and just the fact that he offered information and denied bcc'ing anyone meant that he did. I avoided him for weeks after that. Finally, when I was able, I acted like nothing happened between us. But, inside, I knew who he was and what he was capable of. I never trusted him again. I used this incident as a learning experience. I learned that presenting him with my views was not productive and did not change his behavior. So I did my job to the best of my ability and tried to avoid his personal rants as much as possible.

Different races in the workplace are an opportunity to learn and understand.

When I worked in downtown D.C. as a federal employee, I was taken aback at the obvious difference between black and white employees. The white employees held the higher-grade jobs; many were political appointees or high-level career employees. The black employees held lower-grade jobs, mostly administrative-type positions. The black people all knew each other and had their own network. They had each other's back. They greeted each other when passing in the hall. The white people all competed with each other and worked in fear of losing their jobs or being ostracized. Many were obnoxious to other employees and tried to discredit them.

I had an African American secretary, Doris. Doris could barely afford to work. She had three children in a wide age range. Working meant finding child-care for the youngest and paying for transportation to get to work. Neither was an easy thing for her to do. One time she borrowed ten dollars from me just so she could catch a bus and get home. Of course, I never saw that ten dollars again, but at least I helped her in just a small way when she needed it. When I needed furniture of any type, she would find it for me in surplus in the basement because she knew the guy (black) who managed surplus furniture in the basement.

Four of my twelve employees were black women. Three of them were in technical positions—two were web people, and the other was a member of the network team of all white men. I heard from the men that LaShon was not pulling her weight. I began to watch her more closely. Her routine was to come into her office in the morning and then disappear for the rest of the day until it was time to go home. The premise was that she was on calls to resolve technical issues other employees had. But I came to learn that she was helping her friends (black) only and hanging out with them. So I began mentoring her. I requested that she come in to see me every morning when she got to work so we could go over what needed to be done that day. She was absent a lot, and I began to suspect that she was falsifying her timesheet. So I began to take attendance of all my employees every morning. When they got to work, I put a check by their name. I had to take attendance of all my employees because I could not single out LaShon. The other two technical black women employees objected to my taking attendance every day. They felt like they were unfairly being scrutinized. They reported it to my supervisor, the agency CIO. My supervisor, his Deputy, and I had a discussion about it. The CIO said I best stop the practice. I said, "I've never seen anything like this. This is a matter of the black folks against the white folks." I was trying to express my amazement at the large elephant present in that building that no one acknowledged. Instead, both my supervisor and his Deputy shamed me and said, "Don't ever talk like that again!" I wasn't sure what I did wrong except to state the obvious. But that was not allowed, not even with the people I trusted most—my supervisor and his Deputy. The "white folks," as I called them, did not deal with the black folks and their issues. As long as the black folks stayed in their low-grade jobs and did not cause trouble, all was well. If they did cause trouble and filed an EEO complaint, they were promoted to a job they did not know how to perform. This caused even more angst among the blacks and the whites because no one mentored the blacks to enable them to perform in higher-grade jobs.

So were the whites accepting of their differences from the blacks? I would say yes. But that was not enough. So I did my part. I continued to mentor LaShon. I tried to gain her trust by talking with her heart to heart. I told her that, in her world, she had not just one strike against her but two. She was a black woman working on a white-man team. She had to hang out with them and learn from them. She had to try harder to perform and do a good job so that she would be accepted. I worked with her every day. But, one day, she disappeared from work and never came back. I was told by the agency doctor that she had a legitimate illness where she would become catatonic and unable to perform. So I understood then why she was not responding to my coaching. To top it off, while she was away, she filed an EEO complaint against my Deputy and me. In it, she claimed that I said she had two strikes against her because she was a black woman. She took out of context what I said in confidence and turned it into an act of discrimination. After two years, she was finally fired by the government—a rarity. Her complaint was dropped.

I concluded from that experience that existing in each other's worlds is not enough. We must work to understand where each other is coming from and help each other succeed. LaShon was afraid that if anyone knew she had a mental illness, she would be fired (which I don't think is true, but that doesn't mean she did not fear it). I understood why LaShon filed an EEO complaint—to save face with her friends and to cover up her illness. She wanted to fit in, but she just could not. She was not able to perform in the position she was hired. She needed a counselor who could help her find a job for which she was suited and that she could perform with confidence. That type of thing did not exist at that time.

Public radio recently featured a story of a blind man, Michael, growing up. He was just four years old when he was diagnosed with eye cancer, and both of his eyeballs were removed and replaced with fake eyeballs. As a toddler, he was always climbing on things in the house—bookcases, staircases, furniture, and so on. After he lost his eyes, he continued climbing things, including trees and fences. One time, two policemen brought him home to his mother. They had found him climbing a neighbor's fence. The policemen told the mother that they were concerned for his safety, implying that she should keep a closer watch on him. But his mother, who had experienced marriage to an abusive, controlling partner, was determined not to control her own son. She was determined not to put limitations on him that restricted what he could and could not do. By the time he started grade school, he had figured out that he could assess his surroundings by sound waves that occurred when he made a clicking noise with his tongue against the roof of his mouth. One of Michael's teachers at the local public school he attended called his mother to tell her that he needed to stop making the clicking noise because "it wasn't socially acceptable." His mother stood her ground and told the teacher that the kids would have to get used to it because that was how he was able to function in a sightless world. Michael continued to learn and grow to the point that he found he could ride a bike by clicking more frequently. His mother gave him a bike one Christmas. Everything was going well at school for him until another blind boy moved to the school. The new boy, Adam, had a totally different experience as a blind child up until then. He had not learned how to click and, thus, be aware of his surroundings. Someone had always guided him everywhere and done things for him. He said, "I don't know why people always did things for me; they just did." When he joined Michael's school, he was constantly running into walls and other things since no one escorted him everywhere. Teachers and students lumped Michael and Adam together as the "blind kids." Michael resented it because he was so different from Adam. Michael began to make fun of Adam. Michael continued to display disdain toward Adam until they finally went their separate ways in junior high school.

What Michael found was that people's concept of what blind people could or should do was limiting and affected his ability to function in society. As a child, his mother battled people who wanted to limit Michael's activities "for his safety." Michael even found the Association for the Blind did the same thing. The radio narrator gave the example of a man who had worked for a manufacturing company. An accident occurred in which the man lost his eyesight. But because of his work ethics, the company suggested he learn from the Association for the Blind how to his job without sight. When the man sought assistance from the Association for the Blind, he was told, "Oh no. Blind people can't do that." He was given a job making pencils and mops instead. Michael, too, ended up working for the Association for the Blind because he was not given opportunities elsewhere and because the Association for the Blind said that that's what he should do.

To me, this is a prime example of why we need to practice emotional intelligence and understand and accept people's differences. Society's underlying discriminations place limitations on people's concepts of themselves and on what they can and can't do. In this case, it was a blind person who was the victim of society's discrimination. But the victim can be anyone who is different. It took courage for Michael's mother to stand up to society's attitudes toward blind people and to allow Michael to do whatever he thought he could do. When there were accidents, such as the time when Michael rode his bike into a telephone poll and knocked out his front teeth, it took courage for her to suppress her fear for him and allow him to keep riding his bike. Her courage instilled courage in Michael. He didn't look at himself as a blind person. He didn't place limitations on himself. We need to do our part in society not to lump people together or apply labels or categories to them. We need to accept that everyone has unique assets and capabilities. Instead of limiting them, we need to encourage and support them. When Lauren worked for me and I asked her to do something, at first she would tell me, "I can't do that!" I responded by telling her she *could* do it; she was highly capable of doing anything she set her mind to doing. Then she did it and did it well. So we constantly have to ask ourselves, *Am I judging someone by my own standards or beliefs?* If the answer is yes, we need to let go and, instead, give the other person encouragement and support in what they do or want to do.

Coincident with the feature on Michael was a feature on the study of rat behavior. The premise was that rats behaved as humans expected them to behave. Two study groups of people were given two sets of rats to help through a maze. One group was told that their rats were super intelligent; the other group was told that their rats weren't too bright. The rats, however, were all the same. The rats that were given to the group who were told they were superior completed the maze faster. The conclusion was that the rats behaved as the people thought they would behave. If this is a consistent truth, it would give even more credence that people, too, will behave as we expect them to. If we give them the benefit of the doubt and believe they will excel, they will.

Spirituality

Spirituality is a consciousness of the soul and the spiritual world outside the practice of religion. It is learning and understanding what the soul is and needs for happiness. It is the practice of honoring and feeding the soul. Spirituality hopefully leads to enlightenment and awareness. Most spiritual practices include meditation, which redirects a person's thoughts from the mundane, sometimes scary or destructive thoughts that continuously pass through our consciousness. Meditation is a matter of training your consciousness not to think destructive thoughts.

Far along my spiritual path, I read Eckhart Tolle's *The Power of Now* and *A New Earth: Awakening to Your Life's Purpose*. These books summed up all the things I had learned from many other authors about living a spiritual life with emotional intelligence. In *A New Earth*, Tolle said, "Nonresistance, nonjudgement, and nonattachment are the three aspects of true freedom and enlightened living." My grandmother and mother always said, in trying times, "And this, too, shall pass." That is what Tolle is saying. If we realize how transient everything is, we won't fall on our sword for the emotion of the day. Things are constantly changing, including our emotions. What shouldn't change, however, are our principles for living.

My second husband was a type A. He exhibited a common trait of a type A in that he often woke up at two or three in the morning and started thinking about work or other things and could not go back to sleep. I told him that he needed to train his mind to turn off those thoughts and go back to sleep. He scoffed at me as if it I were being ridiculous. But, to me, it was a no-brainer. I had spent my entire life developing thought control. I hit the pillow and fall asleep and don't wake up until either the alarm goes off or eight hours have passed (except for bathroom trips in the middle of the night now that I have been through menopause). That is because I turn off my thoughts when I go to bed. I figure I spent all day doing and thinking the best I could. There is nothing I can do at nighttime when I should be sleeping that would make anything better. I need my sleep to perform at my best the next day. So, although I don't practice daily meditation, I am a believer in it as a method to train your consciousness. I don't have bad tapes that I allow to take over my stream of consciousness such as "you're not good enough," "you can't do it," and so on. I understand that others do have these tapes and recommend that they talk to someone about them and use meditation as a means to control them.

My spirituality is important to me although I do not practice any one religion. My spirituality has grown through the years, and I have had several people help me along my spiritual path. It started in high school when my best friend was chair of the Sodality and I was vice-chair. The nuns kept encouraging us to enter the convent, but both of us said, "No way!" We both ended up getting married. My friend is still married today with three children and six grandchildren. She has had a spiritual director for many years now. I am divorced (twice) and have had no spiritual director through the years. Instead, I read book after book (self-help and spiritual) to help my spiritual growth.

My best girlfriend from high school visited me in Annapolis one year. She said she admired me for growing on my spiritual path by myself with the help of books. She has met with a spiritual director for twenty-five years now, and has been a spiritual director for others for fifteen years. She recommended that I find a spiritual support group. With her encouragement, I joined a spiritual meet-up group where I live. This will help me connect with other people who will support my continued spiritual growth.

As a result of my spirituality, I believe that God, or the Universe, takes care of each of us. Part of our spirituality is to open ourselves to help from God or the Universe. Sometimes "listening" to God or the Universe is difficult. But during times of searching, we open ourselves to messages from the Universe or the spirit to guide us and help us make decisions to carry us further along our spiritual path.

When I was in my forties, I went through traumatic times at work and at home. I would say that that is when I first became enlightened as to the reality of the relationships in my life at the time. The men I worked with were condescending and controlling. When I went home and wanted to talk about it with my husband, I met with the same thing. I divorced my husband because he had an acquisition sickness whereby he kept buying and buying things for himself and did not put our needs or desires as a couple first. He ran up huge bills on multiple credit cards while I was barely able to keep a dollar in my wallet. It was very hard for me to end the marriage, especially since this was my second "failure" at marriage, as I viewed it at the time. It took me several years to get back on my feet. During that time, a coworker of mine introduced me to the books *Conversations with God* and *Course in Miracles* and to Marianne Williamson. I read these books and selected books by Marianne Williamson, and my spiritual development took a giant leap. I read other self-help books and felt encouraged that I did the right thing by divorcing my husband. When I first met Kurt (who I never married), he was also very spiritual and gave my spiritual development another boost. I started reading about many spiritual philosophies such as Zen, Taoism, Buddhism, and even Islam. I really liked the Buddhism philosophy and tried to implement some of its teachings I learned. When I left government employment and became a Program Manager for a private company, I hired Lauren as my Program Coordinator. Again, she gave my spirituality a boost. She is a very spiritual person and introduced me to Hay House Radio and the spiritual practitioners who had programs on the station. She is a member of a Buddhist community. As a result of listening to Hay House Radio, I went to one of Hay House's "I Can Do It" conferences in Toronto. It was a wonderful experience for me. There were all kinds of people there—psychics, healers, people who cured themselves from cancer, regular people like me, and more. I got to hear my favorite medium, John Holland, in person.

Part of emotional intelligence is recognizing that you are part of the great scheme of the Universe and being grateful for your role and your gifts. I see that the Universe, or God, has been so good to me and has taken care of me whenever I needed it—in big things and in little things. It has brought me people when I needed them to boost my spirituality. My spirituality has enabled me to have faith that I will have everything I need when I need it. With this confidence, I can let go of any paranoia or fear and focus on helping and supporting others. I am grateful for everything the Universe has done for me and provided me.

There are many cases where I know the Universe was looking after me. For example, my last task at a federal agency ended July 2015. I wasn't worried about employment because a former colleague of mine had promised me a job in the government as a political appointee. But since he started promising in January and it was already July and nothing happened, I applied for other jobs. Nothing came through, so I worked on my houses. I embarked on projects that required my presence to oversee contractors. When I had finished all the projects I had on my list, it was November. Still no sign of the job I was promised. Then my mother fell and broke her hip and was in rehab for two months before she died. I went to see her in rehab and stopped by her apartment to pick up something to empty her apartment every day. By the end of January, I had everything cleaned out of her old apartment and a new place picked out for her. She never got into her new home in assisted living; she died February 6. I had time to myself to recuperate, and then my friend Mary had back surgery on April 19. I helped her through the post-surgery time by taking her grocery shopping, taking her to thrift shops, helping her start her garden, sitting with her and watching HBO, and so on. Just about the time the doctor told her she could drive again, my friend Lauren had hip replacement surgery on June 21. I took care of her for a week and her dog and cat for two weeks at my home. The week after I took Lauren and her pets home, my best friend from high school came to visit for five days. After I took my friend to the airport, I stained the new fence in my backyard and strained my back. I rested and did basically nothing for a week.

All the while, I had been applying for jobs, and nothing came through. I had a couple takers, but they were waiting for the government to do something. At times I felt that the Universe had abandoned me. But I kept finding pennies on the ground, which I took as a sign that I was not forgotten. I see now why the Universe didn't want me to work right away. I served several people who needed me at the time, including my dear mother, and finally wrote the book I had attempted to write for several years. I did what the Universe wanted me to do. Most of the time I was confident that the Universe would provide me with a job at the right time. At times, when I lost confidence, I would find another penny on the ground; the Universe reminded me I was not forgotten. Of course, there were times that I got so impatient that I could hardly stand it. Usually, during those times, I would make another professional contact in a subtle plea for a job. One of those pleas actually paid off. A year after my last task had ended, I started attending the spiritual meetup I had selected at my friend's suggestion. The intuiter who led the meetup told me that she "saw" that, yes, I would find a job again, but she saw October as the month I would start work. I started my new job the last week of September. Her intuition gave me more confidence and helped me relax more those last three months of unemployment. I immediately was happy with the job duties and the people I worked with and saw that this was the Universe's plan all along. I am so grateful.

Spirituality and conscious care of the soul cause us to seek work in an area where we feel our life's purpose is fulfilled. Studies on what motivates people at work have found that money is not the number-one thing. We seek work where we feel valued and can make a contribution to the mission of the organization we work for. We seek work where our passions lie and where we can open ourselves to love our work and the people we work with. When we don't agree with the culture or ethics of the organization we work for, then it is decision time. How far are we willing to go before our principles are compromised? Or do we already see the writing on the wall and the need to move on? In *A Life at Work*, Thomas Moore said:

> "Spirituality affects our work in three key areas: It leads us to engage in work that give life meaning; it calls on us to do work that is ethical and carried out in an ethical context; and it inspires us to do work that makes a contribution to society."

In seeking my next job, I was interviewed many times. Many of the interviewers wanted to know why I held so many jobs in the past three years. Deep down I knew why. The real reason lies in a spiritual plane rather than the material plane of the land of corporate employment. I could not relate the deeper reason to recruiters. I could only explain in terms of scenarios. So I explained the best I can in material terms and said that the job requirements changed. On a deeper level, in each case, someone had their own agenda that I was not privy to, nor were any of my subordinates. For whatever reason, that someone chose not to share their agenda with anyone. They manipulated the situation at the expense of others. This is a form of dishonesty and disrespect. It is an example of lack of emotional intelligence.

I happened to catch a neighbor in her backyard one day. I told her I was still looking for my next job. That brought the conversation to her job experiences. She is in the same career path as me—IT Program Manager. She related to me that it was getting harder and harder to find a work environment that was not fraught with bosses with their own agendas and who were disrespectful of their subordinates. She had changed jobs several times in the past several years trying to find a healthy workplace. In the meantime, she was taking courses and accepting jobs in her new career field as a nutritionist. The new field was something that fed her soul and something she had a passion for. She and her husband eventually relocated to Cleveland, Ohio, to open a café serving healthy foods. They both kept their other jobs, however, to help cover the costs of owning and operating a restaurant.

Be aware that spirituality is like a marriage. It requires continuous work and attention. You need to keep nurturing it and growing in it. And, no matter how spiritual you feel, there will be times when you feel down and abandoned by God and the Universe. In *Sacred Contracts*, Caroline Myss relates the tests to their conviction to sacred contracts that Abraham, Jesus, Muhammad, and Buddha experienced. All overcame doubts to be true to their convictions. We nurture our spirituality by sharing it with others, reading spiritual books, attending spiritual meetings, attending spiritual services, honoring the Sabbath, meditating, enjoying quiet time in nature, and so on. Whatever we do, we need discipline to establish routines that nurture our spirituality.

In *Everyday Grace*, Marianne Williamson said:

> As we release our need to be "seen," to be clever, to achieve, or to perform, the way is made clear for our inner radiance to shine. In a noisy world, seek the silence in your heart. And through the power of silence, the energies of chaos will be brought back to harmony—not by you, but through you, as all miracles are.

Empowerment

To manage ourselves and our relationships with others, we must first empower ourselves and then others. We must give ourselves permission to love ourselves and others, as well as to treat ourselves and others with dignity. We've all heard the adage, "Trust your instincts." The "gut" tells us what emotions we're feeling. For example, when we feel a loss of some kind, we may feel a "hole" in our gut. If we are experiencing fear, we may feel queasy or sick to our stomach. If we are distrustful, we may also feel a mild queasiness. I have a friend who vomited several times at her wedding reception because she was a virgin and was concerned about the wedding night.

Giving yourself permission to notice what your gut is telling you and to act wisely in response to those sensations is what emotional intelligence entails. I'll never forget the first time I read Scott Peck's *The Road Less Traveled*. I was half my current age and had just ended a long relationship. People who disrespect us, according to Peck, should "just say no." It hit me hard. I can do that? I can say no to disrespect from others? Being a good Catholic girl, I wanted to please everyone and everyone to like me. The thought that I could say no to someone was new and empowering. I took this to heart in both my career and personal life. If I encountered a disrespectful boss in my career, my way of saying no was to move on to another job of better pay and new and different responsibilities. That way I honored myself and kept growing. I did not hold anger inside and did not exhibit disrespect in return for the disrespect I was experiencing. I understand that changing employment is not for everyone, but it is critical that we keep it as an option. We can keep applying for jobs as long as we have one until we find something else we want to pursue in a new environment. In my personal life, if a "friend" lied to me, to me that meant that he or she disrespected me and I let that person go; I quietly ended that relationship.

Recently, I lost one of my two cats. I adopted a second cat as a companion to my senior male cat, Sheridan. She was a two-year-old female named Lily. From the beginning, I noticed Lily did not bond with either me or my senior cat. She was always staring out one of the windows. I knew this was about the last time I should be getting a young cat because I didn't want them to outlive me. I wanted a cat that was affectionate and would hang around me. So, I adopted a kitten who was happy and rambunctious. I figured she and Lily would grow up together and get used to each other. But it didn't work out that way. Lily became increasingly desirous of being outside and began urinating inappropriately inside when she did not have her way. This upset Sheridan and he, too, started urinating inappropriately. I blamed myself over and over for creating an undesirable environment for Lily. But in my gut, I knew that Lily was the way she was because she had been an outside cat and, as she became more and more comfortable in her new home, she was going to make her desires known. I resisted my gut instinct that Lily was simply not a suitable match for our family. I kept proving myself wrong for adopting Mila and creating a chaotic environment for Lily and Sheridan. I needed to give myself permission to honor my needs and desire for a home of two happy, affectionate cats. I wrote down a list of reasons why I should give Lily back to the rescue to find her a more appropriate home. The list made me realize that I had to give Lily up. I cried the morning before the woman from the rescue picked her up and when she put her in the car. It took days for all of us to get used to life without Lily. But, in the end, we all knew it was the best for us and for Lily.

After learning to empower yourself, you are able to empower others--lose your ego and learn the talents and skills of the people that surround you. We then can encourage those people and empower them to use their skills. In the workplace, you will notice that, generally, men more easily display their skills and market themselves. Women, generally, are often less skilled at marketing themselves and can easily become invisible or diminished. Just as extroverts need to give introverts a chance to express themselves and contribute, men, in a male dominated environment, need to empower women to be the best they can be. This goes beyond equal pay for men and women. It is giving women the opportunity to contribute to the mission by using their talents and skills.

I have so many stories and examples of men suppressing my capabilities during my career. The first time I encountered this was when I had an engineer boss and worked side-by-side with another woman engineer. My supervisor was a control freak. His wife called every hour on the hour to receive instructions from him on what to do next. The papers in his inbox kept piling higher and higher for things he needed to take care of, all the while my coworker and I begged for work. My supervisor had to control and touch every task that had to be done. Therefore, our group made very little progress. My coworker and I couldn't stand it. We were so bored! She got married and moved to New Mexico where she started a family and a natural health consulting business. I changed jobs to work for the Program Manager of the Doppler radar program. He empowered me! He supported me and I accomplished SO much! Both he and I were proud of my accomplishments. He deserved much credit, too, because he saw to it that my work was funded and that I had the authority to seek and use the resources I needed to get the work done. Many individuals were pleased with my job, including myself and my supervisor. That was, without a doubt, my best job ever.

The "Me, too" Movement is an effort to make both men and women aware that men and women will no longer stay silent about sexual abuse and harassment. There were examples of men and women not reporting sexual abuse they experienced for years. This did not serve them well. We learned that, if abused sexually, men and women must report the incident immediately even if they live and/or work in a culture where such reports are frowned upon. We must use emotional intelligence to understand the emotions we are feeling and what to do about them, and act sensibly in consideration of those feelings. We must "say no" to the disrespect we experienced and to the person(s) who disrespected us. Our report may save other men and women from experiencing the same disrespect.

Below is a quote from my neighborhood Facebook group describing an incident of disrespect at the neighborhood drug store:

> "Wanted to express the outrage I am feeling about our local drug store manager, Mike. Today is not the first time my family or I have witnessed him being rude to

guests or employees. My daughter went in around 6:30 am and a truck was there. Two men who work there were helping unload it. One of the adult men who, from my educational background and personal experience, seems to be a person with special needs. We have seen him working there several times and he was always polite. He was attempting to carry a heavy crate into the back. The store manager was in the aisle and using the inventory gun; he refused to move when the guy asked him politely. The manager proceeded to yell loudly, "Don't you see me doing something? Stupid, go around. I am not moving." The yelling and belittling went on for a few minutes. The manager, seeing my daughter and people now watching, went into the back. The man he was yelling at looked confused and then embarrassed. Head down, he continued doing his job. A few minutes later, the manager returned with a smile, walked up to my daughter, and asked, "How are you today?" My daughter was, like, "Are you serious?" and let him have it. She told him that no one deserved to be talked to that way and, especially, a person with special needs. He then shrugged, like, "Oh well. If you do not like it, do not shop here." I called corporate already but wanted the community to be aware of how the manager treats the employees. I would not want anyone to apply and have to experience that. If anyone else has witnessed this, please contact corporate. I googled the number."

Numerous people commented that they, too, experienced the manager's yelling and abusing employees. Here are a couple of the comments that followed:

"So glad that you have taught your daughter to stand up to this bully. So impressed with both of you."

"Fear, loss, hopelessness is manifested as anger, unfortunately. I feel it is better to have compassion when confronted with anger, see what I can do to help the situation. Life is the toughest of paths. Extend your hand to others along the way."

What are your thoughts? Ordinarily, I'd agree the second statement was appropriate; it demonstrated the man's emotional intelligence and reserve of judgment. However, considering the manager's track record, I'm afraid I'd agree with the first comment. The manager has been witnessed abusing employees on numerous occasions. Emotional intelligence tells me that compassion and lending a hand to someone who regularly expresses anger toward employees does not work. It is best to report such a manager's behavior to his/her management. A person's workplace does not need to be a toxic environment.

As you can see, using emotional intelligence is situational. We need to learn about and understand the problem. Understanding people, what they can and cannot do, and enabling them and yourself to do things that will make others happy are all part of self-management. If you become jealous of someone's accomplishments, that means your ego is getting in the way and you need to get it in check. Emotional intelligence means being happy for others' accomplishments. It's OK if you admire what they do/did; you can ask to assist them or support them in some way they need.

Dealing with Emotions

Do you know about Maslow's hierarchy of needs? (See figure below). The second box from the bottom is "safety." If you feel secure within yourself, you can start directing your attention to someone beside yourself and "belong" to others. Those who are fearful and insecure—and emotionally immature—can focus only on themselves and their needs. They act out of fear and are more prone to hurtful behavior to others. Spirituality helps us move up on Maslow's hierarchy. It helps us to grow emotionally intelligent. It helps us develop compassion and empathy for others.

Figure 1. Maslow's hierarchy of needs

We all have emotions every day all day. We are happy, we are sad, we are agitated, we are angry, we are lonely, and on and on. Emotions can change on an hourly basis. But it is important how we deal with these emotions. Most of all, know that what you are feeling at the present moment will change in the next moment. That is reason enough not to panic about the feelings you have at any one moment. Marianne Williamson said:

> "Our emotional reality is ultimately our own responsibility." We can choose to be happy in a job that's going nowhere. We can choose not to be angry at someone who has wronged us in some way. We can choose to see the good in someone when their behavior is not lovable." (*Everyday Grace*).

My philosophy is to be open to someone I meet unless or until they give me cause not to. It doesn't mean, though, that I no longer feel love or compassion for them. It means that I can't continue to keep them in my life if they continue to dishonor me. Take for example, the man I dated for seven years. His mental illness caused him to exhibit destructive emotions in spite of the fact that he was taking an antidepressant. After two years together, he told me he wanted to see other women. This hurt me deeply, but I gave him his freedom. He realized how much he hurt me and kept reaching out to me, which tore me apart even more. My boss at the time was a really good person. He told me that I should forgive him if I really loved him and we should get back together. He knew my friend and liked him. I thought about what he said and took his words seriously. However, I knew my friend would never change. If he was disrespectful of me after two years, I had doubts that he could maintain a relationship longer than that. We got back together and celebrated our reunion. But in the back of my mind, I tried to prepare myself that he would again want to see other women. It lasted another five years, but during the last year, he had withdrawn himself emotionally from me and was no longer intimate. It only lasted as long as it did because I kept adjusting my mind-set and expectations. After we split again, I asked myself, did I manifest our final breakup because of my doubting him, or did he just have other designs all along and the breakup was inevitable? In any case, I could not remain in a relationship where I was disrespected. Today I still love him, but I know that we can never be together as a couple. I learned a lot from our relationship, and for that I am grateful.

Buddhism is all about control of the emotions. Steve Hagen said in *Buddhism Plain and Simple*:

> "Recall that everything we see, hear, feel, and think is in constant flux and change. Nothing endures. We long for permanence and as a result we suffer, for we find none. There seems to be only this coming and going, coming and going, this unending arising and ceasing."

The Dalai Lama wrote a book, which I did not read, entitled *Healing Emotions: Conversations with the Dalai Lama on Mindfulness, Emotions, and Health*. That should be a good one.

A daughter of a friend of mine suffered from symptoms of borderline personality disorder. This is one of the worst types of mental illness. It was inherited from her father's side. As a teenager, she had panic attacks and cut her arms. She had scars all over her forearms. She went to a psychiatrist and took antidepressants. But she did not like the effects the antidepressants had on her. She is very bright and a naturalist. So she learned from the psychiatrist what to expect in the way of emotions and how to deal with them. If she felt a negative emotion, she knew not to panic and just ride it out. It would pass. This helped her cope with the ups and downs she experienced emotionally. She is so much stronger and happier today because of it.

One of the many values of meditation, which is part of the reason why many spiritual philosophies promote the use of meditation, is that it allows us to take pause and gain composure. We've all heard about the chanting of yoga, "Ohm." What we are doing is taking control of our emotions by stopping the negative, egotistical thoughts that control them. Once we take control of our thoughts, control of our emotions will follow.

In the workplace, many managers don't understand that when they deal with their connection with common humanity first, they will appeal to and motivate people toward the office's mission. When they suppress or refuse to deal with matters of the soul, morale decreases and demotivation occurs. Accomplishing mission goals becomes difficult. When mission goals are not met, managers panic and implement authoritarian and scare tactics. People become even more difficult to motivate. If a manager should, instead, resort to team building and cheerleading tactics that appeal to employees' souls, they will unite in a common bond to work together toward their common goal. In *Everyday Grace*, Marianne Williamson said, "Ultimately, it's only people who have done and continue to do their own inner work who can effectively lead a competent modern workplace."

Recently there was a spot on television news about the increase of road rage. People actually come to blows in the street after confronting each other about a driving behavior that enraged someone. Every day we hear about someone, usually with some kind of anger and depression, who takes an automatic rifle and kills as many people as he can. These are cases where people are not acting with emotional intelligence. This is why we need to educate as many people as we can about emotional intelligence. Emotional intelligence is dealing with our emotions in a mature way that is not harmful to ourselves or the persons surrounding us. Emotional intelligence assumes that we understand why we are feeling a certain way at a certain time and handle or control those emotions until they pass.

Coping

Different people cope differently with their emotions. For example, extroverts cope differently than introverts. An extrovert derives his/her energy from others and from interacting with others. An introvert derives his/her energy from within. So, whereas an introvert needs time alone to think things through, an extrovert generally prefers to talk to someone to formulate his/her thoughts. Many of the methods of coping with emotions that I describe here are methods for introverts because they are things that you can do by yourself. However, when one experiences a loss through a divorce or death of a loved one, often times even an extrovert finds himself/herself alone to cope with his/her emotions. Sometimes friends aren't available or else tire of hearing an extrovert's continuous expressions of what s/he is feeling. Generally, though, an extrovert prefers interactions with others to cope with emotions.

I use the word "cope" here to refer to methods of dealing with internal issues or external factors such as people who are not emotionally intelligent and who, if we let them, could induce destructive emotions in us. The assumption, of course, is that we have worked on ourselves first, that we know who we are and where we want to go (with ourselves).

Many people don't have the tools or knowledge of how to deal with their emotions or the emotions of others. They cope the best way they can, sometimes with the help of drugs—pills, powder, alcohol, and so on. Many of the women I know had a relationship with a man who was either an alcoholic or a drug abuser. Sometimes the only escape from mental anguish for these tormented people is suicide. That's why it is important that each of us does our part to listen to others and show them compassion. You never know if you will be the one who saves someone from their last resort. That is why it is so important to learn emotional intelligence and teach it to other members of your family.

One needs to realize and remember that, in a capitalistic culture, needs of the soul are suppressed in order to achieve the goal of maximum production. Therefore, one must be conscious of this fact and make an effort to take time to do things to feed one's soul. Examples are meditating, taking long vacations, developing hobbies at home, spending time with friends, decorating your cubicle with plants and family pictures, expressing oneself through art or music, and so on. I have recently discovered meet-ups in my community. There are meet-ups for so many interests that you might have. I learned of the spiritual group I joined from a list of local meet-ups. I liked the people I meet with there and felt I could relate. There were usually new people each month.

While it seems that there is always someone who is difficult to get along with wherever you work, there are also opportunities to meet good people and learn new things. A person can make it a goal to be happy wherever s/he works whenever possible. I once took on a very small program in a federal organization headquarters that no one else took on because it was so small and not very visible. Most likely they felt it wasn't worth the effort. I became an expert in the program and briefed the top managers in my office at the monthly program reviews. After one of my briefings, one of my managers asked me, "Is there *anything* you don't get excited about, Kathleen?" Like the others, he didn't seem to understand how I could get so enthusiastic about such a minor program. But I took ownership of it and gave it my best. My view is like the saying "Anything worth doing is worth doing well." And doing something well feeds the soul. Steve Hagen said in *Buddhism Plain and Simple*:

> "Human life is characterized by dissatisfaction. It's right here with us. This is the Buddha-dharma's first truth of human life. How do we deal with this reality? Should we pretend—or hope—that what we love is not going to die? The awakened self would answer with a decisive no."

Once we realize that our emotions are *caused* by us within our own selves, it is much easier to understand that we can control them. It may take work to understand and control our thoughts in order to control our emotions, but it is totally worth it.

The book by Sylvia Nasar, *A Beautiful Mind*, and the movie based on the book is a story about a brilliant mathematician, John Forbes Nash, Jr. He shared a Nobel Prize for economics in 1994, the year before he joined the Princeton Mathematics Department as a senior research mathematician. He became known for his work in the foundations of modern game theory—the mathematics of decision making—while still in his twenties, and his fame grew during his time at Princeton University and at Massachusetts Institute of Technology. During his rise to fame, he was diagnosed as paranoid schizophrenic. The story describes how John Nash struggled with his mental illness and tried to conquer it without taking medication. He learned what to expect with the illness and how to deal with the emotions. It was not an easy road, and he had moderate success. This road is not recommended for most.

When my last relationship with a man ended, I was emotionally distraught. My whole life changed. It took me a year to recover from the hurt and the changes in my life. Suddenly, so many people that were in my life were gone. I had no one to talk to about how I felt. When I started talking about my feelings to my mother, she said, "Aren't you over him yet?" It was like someone near to me had died. Suddenly, I could no longer talk with him or touch him. My close friends thought, *Good riddance.* But I thought of all the good times we had shared and how much he had taught me.

In a case like this when we experience a life-changing, traumatic event, it is important to achieve a balance between doing and not doing. By that I mean that being quiet and reflective about what happened and what to do next is important. It is important to grieve a loss. It is important to manage our thoughts to stay positive. But too much quiet time and grieving is not productive. Finding and doing something we are passionate about is also helpful.

During times of change and reflection, I read books that helped me understand what was happening to me and how to get past it. Marianne Williamson's book *The Gift of Change* was so helpful to me when Kurt and I broke up. I printed out a couple quotes from her book, framed them, and displayed them in my bathroom so that I would see them every day.

Her words reminded me how precious change is in our lives. When I was unemployed (as a program manager) for a year, I read *A Life at Work* by Thomas Moore. This book told me that we can have multiple careers in our lifetimes and that we need to use our imagination to find our passion. Thomas Moore's book *Care of the Soul* was another book that helped me realize that I needed to take care of myself, and it taught me how. We learn so much from reading. If you aren't into self-help books, biographies or autobiographies of other people are helpful. You can get lost in the lives of other people who have overcome obstacles in their lives and have done some amazing things. Jane Fonda's life, as described in her book *My Life So Far*, affected me greatly. I was amazed by the challenges she had in her life, what she learned and how she grew, and her lifetime commitment to philanthropy. Even reading novels can take us away from the issues of the day, widen our scope, and enhance our imagination.

Journaling

To cope with the emotions, I felt after my last relationship ended, I began writing in a journal. I wrote practically every day. I can now read the journal and see just how distraught I was and how long it took before my outlook brightened. Writing about my feelings was therapeutic for me. But I didn't just stay home and cry and write. I took advantage of my newfound freedom. I found distractions that got me through the year of pain. I did a lot of traveling and explored new things. I took harp lessons. At the end of the year, I listed all the new things I did so I could look back and feel good about coping with an emotional breakup. I felt I had achieved a balance between quiet and thoughtful grieving and doing and discovering.

Traveling (alone or with a companion)

There are many things we can do to cope. Have you heard the expression "Idol hands are the hands of the devil?" It means that when we are not busy doing something (including meditating), we often allow destructive thoughts to come into our mind. The goal, of course, is to manage our thoughts. But until we become masters at that, we can seek other things to help us cope. Two things I mentioned above, writing in a journal and traveling, are good outlets. When I travel, I get outside of my own little world and experience other people and scenery. I like traveling alone because then I can connect with other people that I would not otherwise if I were with someone else. If I travel to the countryside or rural places, I can admire nature and the beauty of the world.

Yard Work / Gardening

I feel comforted when I am outside in nature. I feel connected to the Universe and the rest of mankind. It makes me feel good inside when I see plants I planted growing and thriving. I enjoy nurturing them and caring for them. I enjoy the beauty they add to my surroundings. As you can imagine, I spend a lot of time in my yard landscaping. If I am outside and a neighbor passes by walking a dog, they often say, "Your yard is beautiful." I feel good inside when I get a compliment like that. In Silver Spring, three of my neighbors suffered from depression. I often think that, if only they could go outside and play in the dirt, it might help relieve some of the depression. Of course, that is presumptuous of me, but I still know how therapeutic working outside in the yard is for me.

On the other end of the spectrum, I have had friends who had to be doing something all the time. They could not stand to be alone or idle. I often wondered what they were running from. One friend was constantly traveling. She would even travel to places she had been before just to get away. I wondered why she didn't find happiness within herself and settle down in a nice place to live. Another friend was always thinking of and doing projects. It seemed like, at times, she would even make work for herself, doing things the hard way, just to keep busy doing something. I wondered what she was afraid of.

Music (alone or in a choir, instrumental group, etc.)

Another method of coping is listening to or playing music. Music is another way I feel connected to the rest of mankind. I think of the singer or members of the band and all the people it took to produce that song or album. Some melodies really grab me. Some songs have lyrics that I can really relate to. Anyway, when I listen to music, I don't feel alone, and I feel uplifted and full inside. Playing instruments is another help. It is a challenge and gives me a feeling of accomplishment when I can play a song all the way through with few or no errors. I grew up playing the piano and have added the Celtic harp to the instruments I play.

Exercise/Walking (alone or with others)

And then there is exercise of any kind. Of course, working outside in my yards is good exercise. But other types of exercise that increase your heart rate are good. I like to bike and kayak. For people with a lot of testosterone or anger, kick boxing or boxing a punching bag is great for letting go of that anger. Even pounding sand is good for that! I finally broke down and joined the local athletic club. It is an opportunity for me to use many different machines and meet new people while I am doing that. If the weather permits, I prefer to take walks or ride my bike outside. If it is too hot or too cold, I use the treadmill at the athletic club.

Sports (alone or on a team)

And there are sports. Playing golf, tennis, basketball, and so on are all outlets. I met and became friends with two women I met in my tennis group. Spectator sports can be therapeutic, too. People can get lost in watching a football game and are moved when their team wins. Computer games are enjoyable. I play Mahjong whenever I have a moment between activities.

Owning a Pet

If you don't want to go it alone, adopt a pet. You are giving an animal a loving home and are getting a constant companion in return. I have had a cat, mostly two cats, my entire life. They are my family, and we treat each other with love and respect. You can work on understanding your pet's wants and needs; all you have to do is listen. They don't talk, but they let you know what they like and don't like.

Social Media

I have a couple friends who are on social media continuously. One friend posts most of her activities on Facebook. She likes to see who "likes" what she posts. She once chastised me (not seriously) for not "liking" something she posted. So I am now more attentive. My other friend loves to follow politics. Election year 2016 was her year. She argued with party opponents on several different social media. You have to have a thick skin to do that, however, because several opponents resorted to name-calling and tried other ways to discredit her. She kept in there, though. One thing,

I noticed, though, is that neither of my friends ever feels alone. Both are single women. When they are alone, they just get on social media and are connected to any number of other people.

Art, Crafts, Hobbies (alone or with a craft club, art class, etc.)
Hobbies are therapeutic. Whether it's arts and crafts, painting, sketching, sculpting, volunteering at the library, whatever, hobbies are an outlet and an expression of our interests. Many self-help books tell us to identify our passions and then follow them. Other books tell us to be passionate about what we are doing—serving people at a local restaurant, fixing cars, and so on. Following our passion or being passionate about what we do is a sign that we are feeding our soul.

Go off the grid occasionally!
I usually avoid malls at all costs. But one morning I went to the mall to buy something for cooking that only a kitchen utensil store would have, and the only place to find a store like that was in the mall. I arrived at the mall before the stores opened. It was very peaceful, and I walked around looking for the store I needed. I realized that I didn't have my cell phone with me. I thought, *How freeing it is to be in a peaceful environment and not be tied to interruptions from my phone.* That's why I like flying in an airplane--I am in a quiet, contained space high above the rat race below. My thoughts go wild.

One of my most memorable experiences going off the grid was when I worked in the Doppler radar program. It took over two weeks (unusually long) to get through the test and acceptance of the Doppler radar at Reno, Nevada. It was a difficult test since it was the first dual system. The two-plus weeks included a middle-of-the night call to me to tell me the system failed. When the test was over, I was relieved and wanted to celebrate. After the owner signed the acceptance form, I headed for Yosemite National Park. I arrived there just before sunset. The landscape and rocks all had a colorful glow. By the time I headed down into the canyon, it was dark. (It was Halloween night). I descended the canyon with hairpin turns very slowly and carefully in pitch dark. When I arrived in the canyon, I looked for signs to direct me to a place to stay overnight. I came upon the lodge. It was a warm, glowing light in the midst of complete darkness. I walked in and smelled pine and redwood and took in the glow of the fireplace. When I asked for a room, they said they were full. I thought, *Uh oh*. But then they offered me a (expensive) room in which the heater wasn't working. I took it; I didn't need a heater with the comforter that was on the bed. I stayed overnight and experienced the same surroundings in the light—much different! There was no cell phone coverage there. When I was finished decompressing and on the way to the airport the next afternoon, I called my counterpart for the prime contractor. He said, "Where have you been? I have been trying to reach you!" I grinned and said, "I know. I went off the grid!" I will never forget the feelings I had with that experience.

Writing a Memoir

Writing this book has been therapeutic for me. I know that many people are not inclined to write self-help books or even read them. But writing about your life can put things in perspective and put explanations into words that you would not otherwise verbalize. I just picture myself talking to someone that I want to help, and that motivates me. Writing about your life or family can be a thing of value to children and grandchildren. I've been encouraging a former neighbor to record memories of her childhood and parents for her grandchildren. Eventually, those stories will mean a lot to them.

Prayer/Meditation (alone or with a prayer group/Bible study/ spirituality discussion group, etc.)

Have you ever noticed that how your day begins sets the pace for the entire day? If you oversleep and rush to get ready for work, you miss the bus and then you get angry. You start the day off being angry at whoever shows up next. All because you did something to yourself that did not show yourself love—rushed to make up for time lost oversleeping. And what about those mornings you wake up, have coffee, and read the news. The coffee gets your adrenaline going and you get agitated at something you read in the news. It takes a while for the caffeine and the agitation to wear off. In the meantime, you get angry at the slightest provocation. So what if we begin our day by being kind to ourselves? If we take five minutes to meditate or just sit in reflection, we can raise ourselves up above the hustle and bustle of the morning to focus on our many blessings and the happy thoughts they bring. We can even take this time to pray for strength and courage during the day, or whatever is relevant for us at the time. More than five minutes is even better. The important thing is to start the day with a positive attitude and serene, insightful outlook that we can share with others and that will create good things to happen throughout the day.

Nurturing Your Spirituality

One of the most important things you can do to feed your soul is to tend to your spirituality. Spirituality is recognition of your soul and doing things that make it happy. Some people join and practice a religion. Practicing most religions usually provides weekly opportunities to meet with other people to honor a spiritual entity greater than themselves, such as God, Buddha, Mohammed, and so on. At those weekly meetings, you pray, listen to inspiring words, and sing inspiring songs. But you don't have to practice a religion to be spiritual. Meditation is a form of practicing spirituality. You can also read spiritual books, attend spiritual meetings, take a walk in nature, do a good deed for someone, whatever uplifts your soul. The important thing is to listen to your soul. It will tell you what makes it happy.

Reading about How Others Have Learned to Cope

When I retired from the federal government, as a going-away present, my boss gave me a book entitled *Don't Let the Jerks Get the Best of You* by Paul Meier. I thought it would be kind of a novelty book with some cute advice. Instead, I found it a really good book with a lot of practical advice. Some of the chapter titles are:

- "It's a Jungle Out There, and It's Full of Jerks!"
- "Meet the Enemy—He Is Definitely Us"
- "Why Not Sing Your Own Song?"
- "You Can't Stuff Your Anger Forever"

Meier tells you how to recognize the jerks of the world and how to stop enabling them.

Losing a job can be traumatic. I have experienced the loss of a job several times in the last several years. If it takes a while to get another job, it can deflate your confidence and make it even harder for you to recover. It is important, though, that you remember that you are still the same person that you have always been. Your first job is to be the best you can be. The rest will come. So it is best to take the time to work on yourself or something that will benefit you and others. Things happen throughout our lives to teach us humility and build our character.

Meet with a Friend or Professional
It is important that we seek help when we feel stuck, oppressed, or depressed. Sometimes we just need someone to encourage us in a time of need. Just like my friend's daughter who learned what emotions to expect and how to handle them, we can all learn some tips from others in our time of need. Whether it is a psychiatrist, a psychologist, a counselor, or a spiritual director, all are trained in how to deal with our emotions and can teach us how to deal with them, too. Or maybe the insights of a friend are enough. We can also find books are our friends. I phoned a buddy who was also a cat lover/owner when I was struggling to heal from the loss of one of my cats. Her empathy at the time was invaluable to me.

Summary
Since we spend a lot of time alone (or in our own head), we best be happy with ourselves so that we can enjoy this time. How do we become happy with ourselves? There is advice everywhere on what makes us happy and what happy people think and do. Here are my thoughts in the light of emotional intelligence:

- Decide on what principles are most important to you. For example, I told you my top principles are honesty and responsibility. There are others like respect for others, support for others, and so on. But I picked my top two, which can lead to other things.
- Ensure that each day you uphold those principles without compromise.
- At the same time, continually look for ways you can grow spiritually (soul) and emotionally (feelings) and practice new ways you can exhibit your growth with interactions with others.

- Surround yourself with people that support your growth spiritually and emotionally and do not surround yourself with people who suppress your growth in your life.
- Figure out what you like and want to do and do it.

I believe that just these five things will help you to love yourself and others and show yourself and others compassion and empathy.

Connecting/Fitting In

We must never forget that we are connected with the rest of humanity. Those of us who do not choose the monastic life of discipline and spiritual focus do not find happiness when we are disconnected from others. Sure, many choose to live in isolation, but it is usually out of fear—fear of being hurt or rejected again. It is like my neighbor across the street explained to me when I asked why she didn't get another dog since she loved animals so much. She said that she couldn't stand the pain of losing another dog. Her last one died in her arms. I thought, *So you are going to deny yourself the joy of a dog because you fear losing him?* It didn't seem like sound reasoning to me. But I know that there are people who rationalize not seeking new friends or pets for this reason. Because of their fear of loss, they are denying themselves the happiness of connection and companionship. To me, this is a good reason to get over our fears. Our lives consist of a series of relationships that come and go. We need to enjoy the connection while the relationship lasts. We need to experience the happiness of connection while we can. (At the same time, I recognize that, as we become older, caring for a pet becomes more difficult and, sometimes, is just not possible.)

As human beings, we all have the urge or need to relate to someone else or to numerous other people. Fitting in or belonging is important to us, especially when we are young. As we age, we realize that it is harder and harder to find people that are just like us that we feel comfortable being with. Fitting in or belonging becomes less important. We care less what others think. And we find ourselves spending more time alone. This is all natural in one's life cycle.

A basis of emotional intelligence is our sense of connection with every other human being in some way. Emotional intelligence is having a sense of community at multiple levels. It motivates us to raise our consciousness from ourselves to others. We have a small community of friends that we know well. But we live in a neighborhood, a city, a county, a state, a country, the world. Modern technology enables us to connect and relate to community on all levels. We learn of the pain of people in countries at war, the victims of natural disasters, persons with diseases and illnesses, and so on through the media. Sometimes a particular instance of pain moves us to want to respond with empathy and help in some way. This urge to help moves our interests from self only to another person or a group of persons, whether we know them or not. Helping our fellow man in some way makes us feel connected and fulfilled, having made a contribution to society or community.

National news occasionally reports stories of people moved to raise money for a cause. A young boy moved by the news reports of lead in water in Flint, Michigan, started raising money for and collected bottled water to send to the people in Flint. A man moved by the news reports of immigrants leaving Syria with barely the clothes on their backs started collecting shoes and clothing to send to immigration camps in various countries. And then there is Doctors without Borders. All of these are examples of people with emotional intelligence and a sense of connection to humanity. People who are disconnected from others experience pain in some form, whether it is the pain that narcissism brings or just plain loneliness.

During the 2020 pandemic, some people claimed that wearing a mask violated their right to personal freedom. This relates to what Viktor Frankl claimed. He stated that liberty is only one side of the equation. The other side is responsibility. As members of a society, we have responsibility to that society. We are responsible for safeguarding ourselves as well as our neighbors against COVID. COVID caused lasting health issues for many and many people died.

In addition to our personal life, our work life is an opportunity for connection to others. At work there are several people that we work with every day and others that we occasionally come in contact with. We also have connections to the organization as a whole. We have connections to the missions of those organizations. If we have a passion for those missions, we are feeding our souls in our work lives. Emotional intelligence allows us to understand and accept each person's individuality and differences.

Our understanding and acceptance of the people and organizations we work with will prevent us from letting our emotions or personal agendas get in the way of the mission everyone is working toward. Of course, there is usually at least one person who is difficult to get along with wherever you work. If that person is allowed to destroy the sense of connection everyone has with each other and is destructive to your peace and sense of purpose, then it is decision time—decide whether the situation can evolve into an environment that is more suitable to your needs or whether you need to move on to other work opportunities. If you are a manager and can decide who your team members are, you might consider reassigning or terminating the difficult person in the group. Your ultimate goal is to love your work and the people you work with.

In today's capitalistic, mobile society, it is not uncommon to change jobs every one to three years in private industry. Sometimes you may move to a different part of the country in a different micro-culture. To be effective on the job, you need to fit in immediately and find commonality between you and the other employees in the office. You need to be flexible enough to live and grow in different environments.

In elementary school, although I didn't fit in with the majority of other girls, I had a few close friends. In high school, however, I found the majority of girls were like me. It was much easier to grow and enjoy doing it. I slimmed down and became more outgoing. It was easy to entertain the other girls and make them, and myself, laugh.

It took me many years in the work world, working for the federal government, to realize that not many people are like me. I took to heart what I was taught by the nuns in elementary school and an all-girl Catholic high school—always keep learning and growing, striving to become more and more God-like. In the work world, I found that fear causes many people to stop focusing on learning and growing but, instead, to focus on how to keep their jobs, look good, get ahead, and make more money. But I also found that reality works against them. Without a good education and much training in key tools like communication, leadership, and management, it is hard to get ahead and make more money. In the government, people are moved into different jobs a lot, depending on the need at the time. Many people end up in jobs they are not suited for or don't know how to perform in. Because of their fear, they become hard to get along with or mean-spirited. They falsely reason that, if they are feared, they will hide their own fear. But other people can see through façades. They soon find out if someone is incompetent and unable to perform well in their job. The façade may continue, but everyone is play-acting and not being real.

The story about the Danish immigrants joining ISIS illustrates how much young people want to belong and be accepted by others. Some will go to any lengths to belong, even if it means danger for them. People seek out others that are like them and stick together. Some look for a strong leader to get behind. Some look for a partner who will support them and shore up their confidence.

Before we can give ourselves in a relationship, we have to work on ourselves and rid ourselves of emotional baggage that prevents us from giving of ourselves unconditionally. Having emotional needs that are unfulfilled places unfair demands on the other person in the relationship. The other person is not there to provide our internal happiness or to fix or soothe pain we feel from our past experiences. That responsibility is ours alone. Only by first accepting and loving ourselves can we accept and love another. Eckhart Tolle said in *The Power of Now*:

> "Never before have relationships been as problematic and conflict-ridden as they are now. As you may have noticed, they are not here to make you happy or fulfilled. If you continue to pursue the goal of salvation through a relationship, you will be disillusioned again and again. But if you accept that the relationship is here to make you *conscious* instead of happy, then the relationship *will* offer you salvation, and you will be aligning yourself with the higher consciousness that wants to be born in the world. For those who hold on to the old patterns, there will be increasing pain, violence, confusion, and madness."

Wow! How powerful are *those* words? How many of us seek a partner for happiness sake? I know I did! Twice! I thought that I was *supposed* to get married and make a man happy and he would make me happy. But, of course, those thoughts were a result of the times in which I was raised. Things are changing, somewhat anyway, today. I was hurt and disappointed when my husbands failed to consider my and our happiness and only theirs. And their happiness consisted of ideas and things far different from my ideas and desires. I must admit, however, that, during both my marriages and my subsequent relationships, I grew tremendously. I realize now that they were an integral part of my life's path and growth. They were meant to be. Breaking off those relationships was extremely hard for me. I had always thought that relationships were for keeps. But, through the years, I learned that people come and go in our lives to help us along our life's path and provide us what we need emotionally at the time.

Family

Many families are dysfunctional. Sometimes there is one sibling who fails to mature emotionally and causes havoc in the family; sometimes there is more than one. Sometimes it is the parents who are emotionally immature. The result is that the family cannot function as a loving, nurturing unit. It becomes every man for himself. Sometimes parents or siblings can be too controlling or meddling. Then escape becomes the operative word. People with a dysfunctional family must try harder to find the help and the training they need to grow emotionally outside the family unit. At the same time, they have to overcome the destructive behavior they learned from family role models and emotional baggage they collected from bad experiences.

Also, there is emotional baggage that you carry from your childhood with regard to your parents and even your siblings. My friend Kurt's mother lived to be ninety-four. I first got to know her when she was in her late eighties. I bought a condo in the same complex as hers in Florida. When I went down to the condo to stay, I immediately got into the social rhythm of her and her friends. Wednesday evening was happy hour at Mango Maddie's. Friday night was happy hour at the yacht club. Sunday morning was brunch at the yacht club. The rest of the days and evenings were opportunities to do anything else. I found Kurt's mother to be a charming, fun-loving lady. But I gradually learned that her four children did not visit her very often. I got vibes that they were amazed that I loved her so much and wanted to be with her. I began to realize that there were hard feelings from her children left from their childhood days. Their father had a mental illness and was abusive to the rest of the family. I believe that the children resented the fact that their mother allowed their father to abuse them and did nothing about it. I knew, from my own mother, though, that in that era, women did not feel economically free and instead honored and obeyed their husbands. As an objective bystander, I can objectify what she was and did as a younger person. I can also understand why her children would feel the way they did about her. Although she was a friend of mine and I accepted her as she was at the time, I also acknowledged that her children had known her a lot longer than I and saw her in a different light. I accepted their viewpoint and didn't judge them for it.

I once worked with a woman who frequently said negative things about her mother and acted agitated and frustrated with her at the office. To my coworker, her mother was always saying and doing things that sent her into a tizzy. Then, at other times, she would talk about things that she and her mother did together in a loving way. I often wondered if she just accepted that her mother was different from her and talked to herself to calm herself after her mother said or did something to upset her if that would prevent her from her emotional outbursts at the office over her mother. On the other hand, I wondered if that was just her makeup to vent in an extroverted manner, using her office coworkers as an outlet for her frustration. If that was the case, we would predict that she would feel better after she vented.

Different Age Groups and Generations

As humans, we all want to be accepted by others and liked by other people. But when you think about the fact that each of us has a unique life's path, you might realize how it gets harder to fit in as we age. When we are in elementary school, we tend to gravitate toward children who have the same type of parents as we do and who hold the same values. In high school, we are growing and having our own thoughts and desires and gravitate toward other children who think like us. But high school is the last time we go to school in our own neighborhood with children from similar backgrounds as us. When we go out into the work world or go away to college, there is a larger pool of people with different backgrounds and who think differently than we do.

I learned a lot by experiencing my mother's aging process as well as that of my good friend's mother. I asked myself a lot of questions as my mother changed with age. For example, I heard that there was a tendency for people to put a parent in a home and visit them less and less. I heard that old people are lonely and a lot of times rejected. When my mother reached ninety-nine, I saw why this happens. By that time, my mother could barely hear (and refused to get hearing aids) and see (she had macular degeneration, and there was nothing eye doctors could do for her anymore), and her world was so small since she didn't get out any longer, except for doctor appointments. She could no longer relate to anything I did. She never gave up being my mother and gave me advice that by that time was not even relevant. I had to yell everything I said to enable her to hear me. If I told her I did something or was going to do something, she had a reason why I should not do or have done it. As a result, I began to visit her only reluctantly. When I dropped off her groceries or picked up her laundry, I did just that and left right away. It was much easier for me to go home and talk to her on the phone. Her phone had assisted hearing equipment on it. That way I didn't have to yell during the entire conversation. I felt more relaxed with not having to yell and didn't feel as threatened by her continual advice. I called her every day during the week and three times on weekend days. So I began to feel bad that I used to condemn people for abandoning their parents in homes. It isn't easy. I justified it by telling myself that my mother was always independent and had her own friends. Even at ninety-nine, she had her own friends at the apartment building. I thought it was important that they provided her the friendship she needed since our relationship always reverted back to mother and daughter where the mother is all-knowing and could do no wrong. (I attributed this to her German heritage. Her mother was the same way). I thought it was important that she had friends who she could relate to and they with her. When I acknowledged the age difference between my mother and me and the generation gap, I found it was best not to judge her or argue with her. I accepted her opinions and advice and considered them when making decisions. I knew my mother had learned a lot about life and people, so I did not disregard what she told me to do or not to do unless it had no application (since she had never experienced some of the things I did). I recognized that my mother cared about me and what happened to me, so I chose to treat her gently.

Technology

Is today's technology really helping us to be more connected and, therefore, feeding our souls? As I see it, there is limited connection, and the connection is not feeding our souls. The technology is not providing us with what we long for—a feeling that we are understood, accepted, and respected for who and what we are. It seems that much of the time that we post an opinion, there are always many people who disagree and, sometimes, get nasty about it. Posting things on social media sites is a form of output. We are putting things out there that may or may not be responded to, that are responded to at the receiver's convenience, and that may, either knowingly or unknowingly, be hurtful to the receiver. Face-to-face verbal communication does not have these drawbacks. If we communicate with a person next to us without the use of a technical device, we exchange words and get immediate feedback to ensure our neighbor understands our intent and meaning. We use tone and emphasis to help express ourselves. We can tell by the receiver's body language how our message was received. This is an important element of emotional intelligence. Emojis were invented to fill in the emotions that e-mail and text communication lack.

I'm sure we've all seen two people at a table in a restaurant, both viewing their cell phones and texting. On the Metro, most people have a cell phone in hand and are either reading or texting. What do you think is the overall effect of these situations? I think that we are staying connected but only to a set number of people. We are having many missed opportunities to interact with other people that might be different from us. For example, the two people in the restaurant may be married and think they know the other very well. But this time together could be used, for example, to exchange thoughts on current events and understanding each other's views on them. The song "Escape (The Pina Colada Song)" by Rupert Holmes was released in 1979. It is a story about how a man, bored in his relationship with a woman, takes out an ad in the paper for someone who likes pina coladas and walking along the beach. Someone answers his ad, and they set up a time and place to meet. Lo and behold, his current girlfriend comes in and says, "Oh, it's you." He is flabbergasted and says that he didn't know she liked pina coladas and walking on the beach. So here is an example of thinking you know someone...

At one point in my career, I lived over fifty miles from work. I took a commuter train to work. I really enjoyed the trip to work because of the interactions with other people I had on the trip. I would usually sit in the same car in the same seat. Other people did the same thing. Eventually, I had train buddies with whom I shared life and work experiences during the trip. How different things would have been if I sat with my nose buried in my cell phone (as people do today), communicating only with people I knew already.

The lesson here is that technology can appear to help us be more connected, but it is limited in the ability to provide us with the emotional connection that feeds our souls. Nothing can replace the feeling of security and warmth that feeds the soul like an intimate relationship where two people share their feelings using words and body language. Technology provides a type of connection, and that type is helpful. But that type communication is not the complete answer for human happiness and contentment. It doesn't provide connection of two souls.

Sexuality/Gender Differences in the Workplace

Historically, it has been considered natural for men to grow up competing in sports. So when they go out into the working world, they compete for jobs and money. This has not been the historical case for women. Women grow up trying to connect with others and nurture relationships. When they go out in the work world, they can easily find themselves victims of men's aggression. At times that aggression is exhibited with sexual connotations. Women's attitude toward sexual connotations in the workplace has changed over the years. I learned to consider it a natural part of men's behavior. Everything reverted back to sex, even in the workplace. There was a man who was the Office Director where I worked two different places when I was a federal employee. He was a braggadocio, and every time he saw me, he would make sexual remarks. My approach was to laugh it off and not take him seriously. On the other hand, there was a younger woman who was a contractor working in a different office. By word of mouth, the people in my office heard that she reported a male coworker who told her she looked nice that day. He got in trouble for his remarks. He was shocked. We all thought that was a bit extreme. The man who made the remarks was not the type to make sexual innuendos.

So different women have different tolerance of sexuality in the workplace. At my age, I have had many experiences where I tolerated sexual remarks and even sexist remarks in the workplace. There was no accountability for it. However, things have changed. People are more aware of what behavior is appropriate and not appropriate in the workplace. At one time, one of the federal organizations I worked for made training in sexual harassment mandatory for everyone because there were so many violations being reported. Women today don't have to tolerate inappropriate behavior and know how to report it to make it stop.

I am a proponent, though, that women should use their assets when applying for a job. Let's face it. We live in a world where appearances matter. If your appearance is an asset, then use it. Of course, it depends on what your assets are and in which industry you are applying for a job. I saw an interview on television with Barbara Corcoran who is one of the Sharks on the television show *Shark Tank*. She said that women should use their assets to get ahead in the business world. For example, if it takes maintaining flowing locks, wearing high heels to enhance your womanliness, or showing a little leg to get you a job or promotion, go for it, if you are so inclined. But always be classy and do whatever you need to do in good taste. This does not mean sleeping with a man to get ahead. If showing a little leg doesn't work, so be it. Try for another job in another place. Once you get what you want, set your boundaries and don't let any man inside those boundaries. When I was younger, I used my womanly charms to get several new jobs. I just made it clear that, when I was there, business was on my mind and *not* monkey business. Usually, the men figured out I was the competition and tried to get rid of it—me. So then I moved on to another job. But at least I made sure I kept the same job status or better. Looking back, I see that men who hired me or worked with me mistook my introverted nature and kindness as weaknesses. They were shocked when push came to shove and I acted with courage, confidence, and skill.

I wasn't prepared for what happened when I crossed the line as a federal employee from a nonthreatening GS-14 to a decision-making manager as a GS-15. All the other male GS-15s viewed me as competition. I viewed them as colleagues and thought we all worked together to accomplish the mission. Wrong! The males generally worked toward their own agendas. I worked for the mission. Sometimes our goals crossed. The men did anything they could to win and get what they wanted. Since I didn't view things that way and didn't act to protect myself, I usually fell victim to the men's schemes to undermine me. I was lucky I was a federal employee for so long. I found ways of moving around instead of getting crushed. I continued to experience this behavior when I started working in private industry. The longest I worked in any one job for any one company was three years. Most of my jobs were under a year. It seemed that I often encountered someone who had some psychosis or was emotionally immature and couldn't stand to see me taking charge and succeeding at my management position. My skills and success brought out my male manager's instinct to compete. That usually resulted in trying to destroy me and/or get rid of me. I must say that the men that allowed and even encouraged me to do my thing were great. I appreciated their confidence in me and did well by them. But there were too many men out there with problems with successful women. It took me a while to realize that it wasn't all about me. It was all about them, and I just ran into them with their emotional and mental problems. And, yes, there are women with emotional problems in leadership jobs, too.

Everyone has a unique life's path. Everyone has a unique spiritual path. The saying "walk a mile in my shoes" means that we should not judge another unless we have experienced everything that the other person has. That is impossible. That person's experiences influence him/her, for better or worse. Most of the time, we do not have enough information about people to judge them after they act in a questionable manner. Of course, we have rules and laws of society so that everyone can live peacefully with each other. Society punishes people who break the laws. If someone intentionally breaks the law of society, the law also dictates the punishment. But in cases where it is not a matter of breaking the law, we need to ensure that we have all the facts about what happened before we judge the people involved.

In *The Gift of Change*, Marianne Williamson said:

> "It is the surrender of a separate sense of self, a claim to
> the totality of life as part of ourselves. Knowing that we

are part of the whole, we shift our perspective from a sense of individual identity to a sense of universal connection. It becomes impossible to act only for yourself when you know that your self includes everyone."

Help from Other People

We all need help at different points in our lives. Either the Universe brings it to us, or we find it ourselves. I have found that people have come into my life and helped me when I needed it most. People showed up for me who brought about major positive career changes. People showed up for me who helped me through challenging personal experiences. And people showed up for me when I just needed a little help on a certain day. The main thing to remember is to be open and ready to receive help at any time. I am referring to a conscious awareness that help is welcomed. Don't be afraid to ask! If you are stuck or down, ask the Universe to send you the help you need. But be looking for it after you ask. Help may not be in the form you expect. So don't rule anything out. Emotionally intelligent people realize they aren't alone in this life and are happy to receive help at any time. Your ego will tell you differently—that only you know what to do or that you are in this alone and no one can give you the help you need. Acknowledge what your ego tells you but let it go.

Have you ever wanted something so bad you kept asking and praying for it over and over and it never came? Then, maybe a year later, you looked back and said to yourself, "It's a good thing I didn't get ___. Things worked out better without ___." Just understand that because we can't see the future, we have to have faith that the Universe will take care of us at all times in our life's path. People will be there when we need them if we are open to them. With this faith, we will find that worrying or getting angry when things don't go as we planned is unnecessary. Things work out for the best in the long run without our control. Life's trials do pass and give way to easier times.

I can cite multiple examples of how people were there when I needed them. When I got married the second time and moved to a new city, I needed a job. I visited a federal office (in the same organization in which I had previously been employed) in a nearby town and met the Office Director. We immediately clicked, and he gave me a part-time job (which eventually became full-time). The job wasn't even related to what my experience was in. I had been in operational meteorology, and the focus of the office was meteorological research. It turned out that he was one of the best bosses that I ever had, and he helped me grow (for almost ten years) tremendously in my career and education. There were virtually no other opportunities for me as a meteorologist at that time in that location. I would have had to commute a long distance to work in my field.

When both the programs I worked in for the modernization of a federal organization were completed, I was placed in a new office for engineers without programs. I got bored quickly. I went down the entire organization directory and called managers who had GS-15 vacancies to ask them if they needed a manager. Some of these introverted scientists were taken aback when I contacted them. One even said nervously, "I don't hire people." I thought it was a little strange when the head of an office said he didn't hire people. No one with open job vacancies offered to even talk with me. I concluded that I didn't need to work for people who were exclusive. I called someone I had heard speak at an IT conference who worked for a federal agency in IT. He said, "Come on in and let's talk." I did, and he asked me, "When can you start?" I said immediately. I was there within two weeks. When I showed up for work, the same man took me to this tiny little room and said, "Here is your office; I will come back to tell you what to do." He never came back. I started reading all the material left behind in that office. There were copies of studies and government laws regarding IT and CIOs. My office was just outside the agency CIO's office. We began to communicate, and gradually I became the Chief of Staff to the CIO. I helped him establish the CIO organization in the agency and documented and distributed the related policies. The short time that I worked for this man (three years), he provided the opportunity for me to grow tremendously as a person and a manager. What I liked is how he trusted me to get the job done. He would say, "Go do," and I would! For my fiftieth birthday, the CIO gave me a framed copy of the agency CIO letterhead which was proof of what we accomplished establishing a new office in the agency. It was an honor.

When I first bought my Annapolis house, I embarked on a project to totally re-landscape both the front and backyard. It just so happened that the man across the street was starting up a landscaping business. I don't know what I would have done without his help. I knew no one else in the neighborhood. Because he was just starting his business, he was available much of the time and stepped right in every time I needed him, and I needed a lot of help. I started from scratch removing anything that was there, seeding a new lawn, and planting many new bushes and trees. As I was reaching my goal and completing my projects, his business started booming, and he had less and less time to help me. Shortly after I finished my huge landscaping project, he gave up his landscaping business to return to his job as a manager for Shoppers Food Warehouse. Coincidence? As I see it, someone above was watching over me. I helped my neighbor get started in his business, and he helped me landscape my new house.

While I was with one of the federal organizations I worked for, I went on a detail to another federal office as part of my requirements for the Senior Executive Service Candidate Development Program to which I had been accepted. When I came back, there was a new CIO. I had been Chief of Staff to the previous CIO. The new CIO was also a bully and had his own designs on who he wanted for his Chief of Staff. I was thankful for that. He didn't know what to do with me when I came back to the organization after my detail. So he offered me up to manage the organization Combined Federal Campaign, which is the annual drive for federal employees' contributions to charities. This was a big deal. The organization had around ten thousand employees. It was customary, when the organization ran the campaign, for the Directors to assign a team of five people: A chair, a co-chair, two financial people, and a public relations/advertising person. The new CIO refused to give me any help. But then there was Debra. I knew her from working with her Office Director and her coworkers. She stepped up to the plate; she and I ran the entire campaign and filled the roles of all five people. Debra and I are still friends today. To me, that was the greatest!

There have been many more cases where someone has been there for me that didn't have such monumental effects on my life. Nonetheless, they helped me when I needed it. When I needed a ride to and from a colonoscopy, Dee stepped up. When I needed a new car and someone to negotiate price, Tom offered. When I needed help cleaning out my condo after the hurricane, Steve was there. When I needed help moving my mother's bed frame out of her apartment, Ellen was there. I will be eternally grateful to all of them. And I have examples of strangers who came out of nowhere to lend a hand. Once, the parking lot was full, so I had to park far away from the stores I wanted to shop in. I ended up buying more than I had planned and had a load too heavy for me to carry all the way back to the car. A woman suddenly appeared and asked if she could help. She walked with me to my car and carried some of the load, then disappeared. Another example is when I used to carry my kayak on top of my car. I could set it up on the car and shove it up onto the roof, but it was pretty heavy. It was much easier when I had help. I used to ask the Universe for help when I was reloading my kayak after an outing. Someone usually appeared.

My friend Mary is a good example of people being there for her when she needed them. I met Mary in one of my short-term jobs at the "office from hell." I was hired by a company to support a federal organization. The environment in the office was set by the Director of the Office, who has some sort of mental illness. Most likely he was bi-polar, but I think he had some other serious issues. He was a tyrant and made working in the office scary. If he decided to pick on you one day at a meeting, you were toast. He would smash you into the ground in front of all of your colleagues. He had a thing about people leaving dirty dishes in the kitchen. He had a contractor terminated for leaving a dirty dish in the kitchen and standing up to him when the Director publicly humiliated him for it in e-mails to the entire office. When I arrived, the Deputy Director of the office had just died of a heart attack. I soon learned why. The poor man did everything in that office. Apparently, he was the only person who had a vision for the office and knew what to do to accomplish the vision. When I got there, no one seemed to know what was going on or what to do. The office seemed in disarray. I can only imagine what the Deputy went through working with his boss. He escaped the more final way. For most people, there was no escape. They all appeared unhappy, overworked, and fearful. There was no joy in their work, no humor. It was the worst work environment I had ever been in.

Part of my job was to hire new people with the other Program Manager to staff up the contract. Evidently, the office had acquired a big budget that year, and though they didn't know what to do with them all, they were hiring contractors right and left. Mary was hired as a web developer. But when she reported for duty, government management determined that she was to reduce security vulnerabilities on the organization's websites. This wasn't one of the skills on her resume, so she had to learn everything as she worked. Of course, this was unfair to her. To me, this indicated that the government managers didn't know what they wanted or how to manage contractors. The government personnel in the office offered her no help or support. They basically ignored her for the first couple months. They assigned a non-professional person who had a reputation for milking the system to oversee her work; he usually "worked from home" and barely worked when he was in the office. He also withheld information from her to maintain his value in the office. Needless to say, she had a hard time doing anything, asking questions, or getting anything done. None of the managers stepped up to the plate and took responsibility for Mary and her work. In their defense, though, they were all full-up on duties and work. I stepped up to guide her and provide her with direction. Of course, the government personnel resented that I did what they didn't do, especially the bi-polar Director.

The result was that Mary and I developed a mutual respect for each other. Mary respected me for helping her and protecting her the best I could. I respected her for her constant can-do attitude. She never let the way the government people treated her get her down, or at least she didn't let it show. What she was able to do, she did well.

After three months, the Director told my company to terminate me. He decided that he was going to change how they did things in the office, and he wanted the company to hire a Software Engineer. This was one of the many unethical acts this man did. If he changed the requirement for one of the contract's key personnel, he needed to tell the Contracting Officer's Technical Representative, who would tell the Contracting Officer, who would modify the contract, who would tell the company program managers. But, of course, this Director felt he was above the law and entitled. He told the president of the company, who told my boss, who told me. My boss felt bad about it, but of course the company wanted to please the government to keep the contract. I prepared my government stakeholders that I was leaving, and they were very supportive. I left feeling good about leaving that toxic work environment.

After I left, Mary and I kept in touch. She continued to provide me descriptions of how terrible it was to work there. She made friends, though, with Miguel, who I also hired in her group. Mary and Miguel worked together on identifying security vulnerability fixes. Eventually, both Mary and Miguel were also terminated. Not a surprise. They both were relieved to be out of that toxic work environment. Both Mary and I found jobs pretty quickly again. As it turned out, we ended up both working in the same building in downtown DC but for different agencies. Mary kept in touch with Miguel, who she got a job for with her company for a brief time to work on the back end while she worked on the front end of a website. They continue to support each other today.

While we worked in the same building, Mary and I started going to happy hours together. Mary gradually told me her story, and I was amazed. I was amazed at what she had overcome to get to where she was today. At the time, she was maintaining a website for the President of the United States (Obama). Mary was from South Carolina. Her parents were uneducated alcoholics who abused her. Mary's only role model growing up was her grandmother, who her parents also abused. Her parents tried to keep Mary from associating with her grandmother, but Mary always found a way. Mary married a lineman who was also an alcoholic. They lived in a trailer and moved from place to place where her husband's work was at the time. Mary's husband also abused her and limited her freedom and resources. When her husband ran off with another woman and charged their trip to Las Vegas on Mary's credit card, Mary was finally motivated to divorce him. It was not easy because she basically had nothing and nowhere to go. Friends helped her get through the separation period and the division of property.

Mary eventually met her "guardian angel." Her guardian angel was in the form of a social worker who encouraged Mary to go to college. Mary was incredulous. She told the woman that she wasn't college material and resisted. She said she wasn't smart enough. But the social worker convinced her by telling her that her test scores were the highest she had seen. She finally did go to a junior college and got an associate's degree in computer science. After she got her degree, however, her advisor told her that she best get a bachelor's degree to increase her chances of getting a good job. Since she had done so well, it was a logical step. Again, Mary resisted but finally agreed.

With the encouragement of her brother who married a woman from the D.C. area, Mary moved to the D.C. area. She worked at several jobs with high salaries supporting the federal government. She even traveled to Alaska and Kenya to support conferences the president held there. And she no longer was beat up by a man who only cared about his agenda. She told me more stories about people who supported her during her breakup with her husband and how the woman she stayed with when she first moved to D.C. was very supportive. I told her that she needed to write a book about her life and how her guardian angels took care of her when she needed help the most.

My motto is "Pass it forward." I try to do things for people when there are opportunities. This honors the people who did things for me. By the way, there is a good movie called *Pay It Forward* that is worth watching.

Conclusion

Simone Biles, during the 2021 Olympics in Japan, was a perfect example of acting with emotional intelligence. Biles, the reigning all-around Olympic gold medalist and one of the most well-known athletes at the games, left the team final after a disappointing vault performance with what USA Gymnastics called "a medical issue." She admitted she was experiencing mental health issues and "the twisties," a phenomenon which temporarily affects an athlete's spatial awareness. Imagine the pressure she was under to perform and win additional medals for the U.S. team! Yet she knew she had to take care of herself; she knew what her mind and body needed. It took courage for her to make the decision not to compete and endure the criticism of some Americans who blamed her for "quitting" and failing the U.S. team. She supported the rest of her team who competed and told them they would do well without her.

Simone Biles addressed her mental health and was cleared for the beam, the least risky apparatus which can be performed with the minimum impact on spatial elements. She rallied in a very short time to take a bronze medal on the beam after returning to the Tokyo Olympics.

I am sure her experience dealing with depression after acknowledging she was a victim of sexual abuse by Larry Nassar, a former doctor for USA Gymnastics and Michigan State University, and the treatment she received, taught her many things about practicing emotional intelligence. She obviously practices what she learned.

The "office from hell" that I described was a perfect example of an environment in which emotional intelligence was neither practiced nor accepted. Employees, both federal and contractor, were not allowed to think or reason on their own. They were only allowed to complete regular or planned technical duties or execute orders from the Office Director like soulless robots. If there was a technical failure of any kind for any reason, those responsible were identified and publicly chastised personally by the Office Director. Those responsible were given short-term deadlines to fix problems and harassed until the deadline was met. Although the Director had little or no experience in software development or implementation and maintenance of software systems, he was the self-appointed expert and oversaw all activities within the office. He alone dictated what systems were implemented when and how. He did not value the experience of his managers who had been doing the work for many years; their input was often ignored. Because of this, his managers were afraid to speak up except to agree with the Director whatever he said or did. His managers were required to brief him regularly on all activities, and he had to approve everything. He let his managers know, in no uncertain terms, if he did not approve something they had done or planned. The Director's plan was to rid the office of as many federal employees as he could and hire only contractors who he could remove at a moment's notice for whatever reason he chose (which is illegal). The employees in the office, including the managers, both federal employees and contractors, were unhappy, fearful, and overworked. They were often disrespectful to each other. People who objected to the tyrannical rule and unreasonable demands in any way were discredited and/or removed. There was no recognition of people as soulful beings with soulful needs. I was not surprised that the Deputy Director died suddenly of a heart attack, seeing what I did when I joined the office. He found an escape. I had seen other toxic work environments before but none this bad. The Office Director appeared to be totally autonomous with no accountability to anyone. If he was reporting to the head of the organization, he was not painting an accurate picture of what was happening in the office. Contractual rules and policies for working with contractors did not apply to him. His Contracting Officer's Technical Representative did as little as possible and then only what the Director told him to do, deeming him virtually useless. The result was that there was a high contractor turnover in the office. This hurt the continuity of the work that was being done.

Everyone's life's path is unique. Different things and people help each one of us in a different way. I have spent a lifetime reading non-fiction books to enrich my life and life's path. So I thought it would be a good idea to share some of the books that really enlightened me that I just stumbled on or someone happened to point me toward. Then you can make a conscious effort to choose the books you want to read that will help you the most. Maybe the summary of key points to living a happy life that I present in *this* book will help you.

My view is that education and knowledge are solutions to some of society's problems. It is a simplistic view, but I contend it would be a start. There are many issues surrounding my simplistic solution, such as what do you do with people who don't want to learn, how do you pay for everyone's education, and who would be covered by education benefits. It is not such an outlandish view since Bernie Sanders, in his 2016 presidential candidate campaign, promised that the government would pay for college education for those who wanted it. But imagine if we were all educated at the same level and shared information that was relevant to living in a diverse society. I believe we would see fewer people lacking in emotional intelligence who try to hurt or harm others. "People learn to the degree they are motivated" (Daniel Goleman, *Working with Emotional Intelligence*). But what if society provided benefits to those who sought education like relief from poverty, care of their children, higher-paying jobs, and so on.

I also believe that people can change their behavior. If someone doesn't already behave with emotional intelligence, s/he can learn it and then adapt his/her behavior accordingly. Of course, this is not without work to use the tools that I have provided here and others have provided in the books listed in the appendix. It takes practice. Sometimes we make mistakes and digress. But if we have the motivation to keep at it, we can implement what we have learned about emotional intelligence from books, experience, and others.

In *The Gift of Change*, Marianne Williamson said, "Our primary function is to stand in the light of who we are and become the people we are capable of being. From that, all good will follow."

The key to changing behavior is to choose and prioritize manageable goals; that is, choose one practice and work on it. For example, if you choose to "become a better listener," you would practice active listening, without interrupting, until it becomes second nature. Then choose another practice and work on that until it becomes second nature. Remember, you have to be motivated and believe that you will benefit yourself and others by your change in behavior to keep up the hard work of behavior change. Once we change our behavior, we are examples for others to let go of the fear and hatred they might harbor. "In order to change the world, we must change the mental lens through which we view it" (Marianne Williamson, *Everyday Grace*).

If you get anything out of this book, I hope it is an awareness. I am talking about an awareness of yourself and other people. If you are aware, you recognize that "I am not the only person in the world" and "I am connected with everyone else." You no longer think that you are the center of the Universe. Instead, you recognize that you are a minute piece of the Universe and mankind within it. You can recognize a person who is aware by his/her actions, some of which are:

- Ask someone for help if you need it.
- Listen to others (active listening) when they are talking with you and don't interrupt them.
- Ask someone why they did something instead of assuming why and judging.
- Do not look at your phone and text when spending time with others or when walking or driving.
- Ask others how they feel, going beyond the small talk.
- When appropriate, respond timely to texts and e-mails sent by others.
- Do what you say you are going to do (when talking to others).
- Ask a friend who told you s/he is moving if s/he needs help.
- Do not eat or drink things your body does not tolerate well.
- Know and understand what you like to do and set aside time to do it (feeding your soul).

All of these things show that you are present in the moment, taking care of yourself and others. You are aware of your surroundings and who is around you. You anticipate the needs of those around you and seize the opportunity to help. When you are walking alongside someone and your head is down with your eyes on your cell phone, you are not aware of your surroundings or the person next to you. You are missing a moment to contribute to that person's life experiences and your own for the better.

When you manage self using the tools I described in this book, you will know that you are doing all you can to grow and be the best you can be as a human connected to all other humans and the earth we live on. You will project a positive attitude toward others, and they will respond in kind. In *The Secret of Letting Go*, Guy Finley provides these truths:

> "Before you can get anything different from this life, you must first do something different.
>
> Before you can do anything different with your life, you must first know something different.
>
> Before you can know anything different, you must first suspect and then confirm that it is your present level of understanding that has brought you what you now wish you could change."

Appendix

Books I Read

Note: Books marked with an asterisk indicate books referenced in this book and those recommended by the author.

No More Nice Girl, Rosemary Agonito
Taking the Path of Zen, Robert Aitken
The Individual and His Religion, Gordon W. Allport
Leadership and Self-Deception, Arbinger Institute
The Highly Sensitive Person, Elaine N. Aron, Ph.D.
The Enneagram Made Easy, Renee Baron and Elizabeth Wagele
Lions Don't Need to Roar, D. A. Benton
Enterprising Women, Caroline Bird
There's Only One of Me Here Today, Sandra Brunsmann
Living, Loving & Learning, Leo F. Buscaglia
Loving Each Other, Leo F. Buscaglia
Our Endangered Values, Jimmy Carter
Job's Daughters: Women and Power, Joan Chittister
Trust Your Vibes, Sonia Choquette
Zen Lessons: The Art of Leadership, Translated by Thomas Cleary
The Art of Leadership, translated by Thomas Cleary
The 7 Habits of Highly Effective People, Stephen R. Covey
Real Moments, Barbara DeAngelis
Secrets About Men Every Woman Should Know, Barbara DeAngelis
Inspiration, Wayne Dyer
Couples: Exploring and Understanding the Cycles of Intimate Relationships, Barry Dym and Michael L. Glenn

The Secret of Letting Go, Guy Finley
My Life So Far, Jane Fonda
**Man's Search for Meaning*, Viktor E. Frankl
*The Sane Society, Erich Fromm
The Art of Being, Erich Fromm
In a Different Voice, Carol Gilligan
Swim with the Dolphins, Connie Glaser and Barbara Steinberg Smalley
He Says, She Says, Lillian Glass
**Emotional Intelligence*, Daniel Goleman
Working with Emotional Intelligence, Daniel Goleman
Destructive Emotions, Daniel Goleman
The Assault on Reason, Al Gore
Think Again, Adam Grant
Mars and Venus in Touch, John Gray
Men Are from Mars, Women Are from Venus, John Gray
**Buddhism Plain and Simple*, Steve Hagen
Games Mother Never Taught You, Betty Lehan Harragan
The Power of Focus for Women, Fran Hewitt and Les Hewitt
The Spirit Whisperer, John Holland
*The Gender Knot, Allan G. Johnson
The Dance of the Dissident Daughter, Sue Monk Kidd
Live in a Better Way, Dalai Lama
An Open Heart, Dalai Lama
The Art of Happiness, Dalai Lama and Howard C. Cutler
Fish, Stephen C. Lundin, Harry Paul, John Christensen
Love is Letting Go of Fear, Gerald G. Jampolsky
Women and Creativity, Dolores R. Leckey
The Trouble with Islam Today, Irshad Manji
Don't Let the Jerks Get the Best of You, Paul Meier
A Life at Work, Thomas Moore
Care of the Soul, Thomas Moore
The Marriage Spirit, Drs. Evelyn and Paul Moschetta
*Sacred Contracts, Caroline Myss
Mahatma Gandhi, B. R. Nanda
Born a Crime, Trevor Noah
Healing the Wounds, David M. Noer

Transforming Fate into Destiny, Robert Ohotto
The Book of Tea, Kakuzo Okakura
The Art of Hanging Loose in an Uptight World, Dr. Ken Olson
Overcoming Depression, Demitri Papolos and Janice Papolos
The Road Less Traveled, Scott Peck
Further Along the Road Less Traveled, M. Scott Peck
Loving and Living, Gerald M. Phillips and H. Lloyd Goodall Jr.
A Whole New Mind, Daniel H. Pink
90 Minutes in Heaven, Don Piper with Cecil Murphy
Reviving Ophelia, Mary Pipher
The Secret of Staying in Love, John Powell
Initiation into Yoga, Sri Krishna Prem
I Don't Want to Talk About It, Terrence Real
Happiness, Matthieu Ricard
Personal Power through Awareness, Sanaya Roman
The Fifth Discipline, Peter M. Senge
Pathfinders, Gail Sheehy
The Awakened Self, Lucien Stryk
Essential Zen, Kazuaki Tanahashi and Tensho David Schneider
You Just Don't Understand, Deborah Tannen
That's Not What I Meant, Deborah Tannen
Eight Habits of the Heart, Clifton Taulbert
Zen Philosophy, Zen Practice, Thich Thien-An
The Ditch Digger's Daughters, Yvonne S. Thornton
Infinite Life, Robert Thurman
A New Earth, Eckhart Tolle
The Power of Now, Eckhart Tolle
How to Avoid Marrying a Jerk, John Van Epp
Conversations with God, 1 and 2, Neale Donald Walsch
Tao the Watercourse Way, Alan Watts
The Spirit of Zen, Alan Watts
Gandhi on Non-Violence, Thomas Werton
Finding Our Way, Margaret J. Wheatley
A Return to Love, Marianne Williamson
A Woman's Worth, Marianne Williamson
Everyday Grace, Marianne Williamson

The Age of Miracles, Marianne Williamson
**The Gift of Change*, Marianne Williamson
Eating the Chocolate Elephant, Mark D. Youngblood

*Recommended

Printed in the United States
by Baker & Taylor Publisher Services